MULTIPLE FAMILY
THERAPY

Other titles in the
Systemic Thinking and Practice Series
edited by David Campbell & Ros Draper
published and distributed by Karnac

Credit Card orders, Tel: +44 (0) 20-8969-4454; Fax: +44 (0) 20-8969-5585
Email: shop@karnacbooks.com

MULTIPLE FAMILY THERAPY

The Marlborough Model
and Its Wider Applications

*Eia Asen, Neil Dawson,
& Brenda McHugh*

Foreword by
Salvador Minuchin

Introduction by
Alan Cooklin

Systemic Thinking and Practice Series

Series Editors
David Campbell & Ros Draper

KARNAC

LONDON   NEW YORK

First published in 2001 by
H. Karnac (Books) Ltd.
6 Pembroke Buildings, London NW10 6RE

A subsidiary of Other Press LLC, New York

British Library Cataloguing in Publication Data

A C.I.P. for this book is available from the British Library

ISBN: 1 85575 277 8

10 9 8 7 6 5 4 3 2 1

Edited, designed, and produced by Communication Crafts

www.karnacbooks.com

Printed and bound by Antony Rowe Ltd, Eastbourne

CONTENTS

EDITORS' FOREWORD

The Systemic Thinking and Practice Series is very pleased to publish its first contribution from the Marlborough Family Service in London. For readers who may not know, this is a pioneering centre that has uniquely applied systemic approaches to work in the community. This highly respected institution has been in the forefront of developing services for child-protection cases, school-based interventions, and family therapy for ethnic-minority communities. But the one service that established its reputation for family work, and has stood the test of time, has been the Family Day Unit, which brings troubled families together to learn from one another.

Readers may be aware that there is a growing interest in the family therapy field to know more about what families can learn from each other. This seems to be a logical extension of the idea that the family has the expertise to solve many of its own problems. If, then, this is true, why not let families support each other through sharing experiences and find new solutions by pooling their repertoire of successful strategies?

This is exactly what the Marlborough Family Service has been doing for years, but now three of their long-standing staff members have taken it upon themselves to describe what they do and to conceptualize why certain approaches seem to work in certain settings, such as the recently established centre in Germany which is based on the Marlborough model. One important feature of this writing is that all of the conclusions are based on years of experience.

The book describes innovative work with a range of family problems, such as marital violence, eating disorders, educational problems, and child abuse. For example, family groups may spend time together reviewing videotapes of their child-rearing activities, or they may convene self-help groups to share responsibility for assisting other families.

We think that readers will find this a refreshing, innovative approach to our most challenging cases and will be enthused by the possibilities that arise when families work together.

David Campbell
Ros Draper
London, 2001

FOREWORD

This short book is written in simple language but describes an extraordinary process: the efficient meandering of the Marlborough Family Service staff, in which they have continually created innovations in the delivery of services while remaining fully committed to the well-being of their client families. In 1976, Alan Cooklin started this process by joining Maxwell Jones's experiments and ideas about the therapeutic community with Bateson's concept of systemic thinking. They were odd bedfellows indeed to use as the base for developing an "institution for change"—a day hospital to work with multi-problem families, who generally attracted multiple providers that, in the end, were ineffective in multiple ways.

When, at the end of the 1970s, I went to London on sabbatical and was invited by Cooklin to consult with the staff, I found an institution ahead of its time. I directed most of my efforts towards helping the staff integrate the family therapy team, inspired by systemic thinking, with the school and Family Day Unit, which was guided more by pragmatic and educational ideas. The staff also borrowed from my work an orientation towards challenge and the creation of therapeutic crises. They transformed this orientation into procedures that served well in some instances and created problems in others—a situation they describe in detail in this book.

During the 1980s, the team re-evaluated their work and invited Boscolo and Cecchin, leaders in the Milan approach, to consult with the unit. That brought the therapist's function into focus, as well as the participation of the professional network as part of the problem, the use of circular questions, and, in general, a more symmetrical relationship between the staff and the patients. What is unique about the Marlborough model is that it did not reject previous explorations as it evolved, but expanded by picking and choosing and by wedding different approaches. As technology improved, for instance, the staff began videotaping family visits to the supermarket—an old idea in progressive education, but applied now to the study of transactional patterns in the family. And an interest in community theatre, on the part of Brenda McHugh, transformed traditional role-playing into mini-dramas between family members and housing officials from the local council. All the innovations have been informed by a respect for family resources and possibilities, a concern for social justice, and considerable energy, among the staff, that bursts into creative responses to challenging family circumstances.

In this book, the authors focus on the utilization of the multiple family therapy model. In integrative fashion, they start with the multiple family technique developed by Laqueur, La Burt, and Morong (1964) and present a rich and complex set of procedures for addressing specific populations in different contexts: hospital wards working with families who have a member with an eating disorder; families with children who have chronic problems at school; court assessments concerning the viability of rehabilitating a violent or abusive family. In discussing these situations, the book is a mixture of thoughtful reflection and detailed procedures: how to conduct home-based sessions; how to link a member of one family with another family—and for what purpose; what curriculum to develop for every day of the week in the Family School; how to use a reflecting team in the hierarchical context of working with families referred by the courts.

I see in this book and its authors the vision of a possible integration of mental health services; a view that involves working in ecological niches, is attentive to context, is morally committed to accessing people's possibilities, and is carried by therapists who search constantly and flexibly for multiple effective procedures.

Salvador Minuchin
Boston

ABOUT THE AUTHORS

Eia Asen, a child and adolescent psychiatrist, is now the clinical director of the Marlborough Family Service. He also works as an adult psychiatrist and family therapist at the Maudsley Hospital and Institute of Psychiatry in South London. After some psychodynamic training in the mid-1970s, he became interested in family therapy, went to work with Minuchin in Philadelphia, and subsequently engaged Luigi Boscolo and Gianfanco Cecchin to take an interest in the work of the Marlborough, resulting in a long collaboration ever since.

Neil Dawson is a psychologist, teacher, and family psychotherapist. He co-founded the Family School at the Marlborough. He has worked as a teacher in mainstream schools. He trained as a systemic therapist some twenty years ago and is now a senior clinical supervisor and family therapy trainer. Together with Brenda McHugh, he has designed and developed training in the application of multiple family systems in schools both in the United Kingdom and across Europe.

Brenda McHugh trained as a drama and English teacher. Through the East London Youth Theatre, which she co-founded, she became increasingly aware of children's family problems and the inter-actions with their schooling. She joined the Marlborough team in 1979 and set up, with Neil Dawson, the Family School. She trained as a systemic therapist some twenty years ago and is now a senior family-therapy trainer. Together with Neil Dawson and Alan Cooklin, she has produced a unique CD-rom distance-learning package called *Family Therapy Basics*.

PREFACE

This book is dedicated to Alan Cooklin, who inspired a lot of the work on which it is based. When he was appointed as medical director of what was then the Marlborough Day Hospital, he quickly introduced a systemic approach to an institution that was at the time dominated by psychoanalytic thinking applied to a public day hospital setting (Mawson & Meyer, 1972). Within a short time, the ideas of a family day hospital and family school were born. The three authors of this book joined the team more than twenty years ago and have, with Alan Cooklin's help, developed the approach. Salvador Minuchin was a major inspiration some two decades ago, when he spent considerable time and energy working with us. His structured and structural input seemed the right antidote for the families'—and our own—chaos! He also read an earlier draft of this book and made many helpful comments. Many past and present colleagues from the Marlborough Family Service have over the years contributed to the evolution of our work, above all Ann Stevens. She headed our Family Day Unit for almost fifteen years, and her clinical skills and creativity remain unforgotten. More recently, we have been stimulated by other teams in Europe who have experimented with our ideas and developed them further, notably the Dresden team led by Michael Scholz.

This book describes the multiple family work developed at the Marlborough Family Service and its application in other settings. Our team has, over the years, written a number of papers and book chapters describing various aspects of our work. However, we had not compiled a systematic account of our work and its organizing principles. Given the recent reawakened interest in multiple family therapy, we thought it timely to produce a book that describes specific projects as well as general techniques and approaches that can be employed when working with a number of families simultaneously. There is no such book in print at present, and we hope that this volume will help fill the gap.

Different as the three authors are, we have a number of specific professional experiences, assumptions, and values in common which are reflected in our approach. First and foremost, we are committed to working systemically in the public sector, mostly with disadvantaged children and adults and families. In doing so, we are constantly made aware of the complexities of family and professional systems and how these intersect. Our orientation is inspired by a range of systemic paradigms, notably a model of active change, emphasis on the "here-and-now", the need for intensity in therapeutic encounters, and, last but not least, the overwhelming importance of context. We are part of a multidisciplinary team, comprising social workers, psychologists, child psychotherapists, nurses, teachers, psychiatrists, and allied workers, all of whom contribute to a multi-perspective and multi-positional stance. We work in an institution, the Marlborough Family Service, that attempts both to employ and to work with persons from many different ethnic and cultural backgrounds. This further increases our awareness of the relativity of assumptions and values, with considerable implications for our clinical practice. In order to explore new and different ideas further, we organize a range of training and teaching events in our institution so that we can learn from others. For many years, we have also been involved in teaching and consulting to many institutions and teams all over Europe, exporting our ideas and reflecting on their applicability to different contexts. The resulting feedback has further informed and changed our practice.

In our clinical work, we believe strongly in working in partnership with children, adults, and their families. This means lowering professional–client barriers and flattening implied hierarchies as much as possible while at the same time acknowledging that there is a significant difference between those who seek help and those who are paid to provide it. When we use the term "family" both in this book and in our clinical practice, we are aware of its serious limitations. "Family" in no way implies a normative nuclear model; we see it as a convenient, though often misleading term, describing multiple and often complex relationships of persons who are involved with one another and share some important aspects of life. We are aware of the many different kinds of families in existence, to do with culture, history, and economic circumstances. In this book, we are also aware of how the term "family" could be misunderstood to imply that there is a real organism such as "a family", with a common mind and coordinated actions. While families are at times capable of behaving as if they were a unitary organism, most of the time—like any other group—they are not. Each family, in whatever way it may define itself, is composed of various members—related or not, distant or close, present or absent. These different members usually tend to have very different thoughts, actions, and emotions. In this book, therefore, the short-hand term "family" has to be enriched by the reader, using some of the above-mentioned dimensions.

Multiple family work involves spending time together for extended periods, including whole days and weeks. This implies forming relatively close partnerships with clients, with more proximity than is usually common in therapeutic work. It results in our daily work being questioned continually by families, and by ourselves. Together with families, we constantly attempt to create and re-create relevant contexts that can be used to promote the possibility of change. This is informed by our awareness that there is a temptation to fit clients and their families into institutional practices rather than the reverse. Much of our work is based on the assumption that all individuals, however seemingly disadvantaged, have resources. This belief—possibly amounting to a prejudice—helps us to encourage families to help one another.

INTRODUCTION

There are three pieces of history—or, as in the currently preferred gender-free term, "three stories"—that predate this book.

The first relates to the experience of an inexperienced and innocent young Senior Registrar (now called Specialist Registrar, or, in the United States, Senior Resident) in adolescent psychiatry working at the new, and many thought "ground-breaking", Young People's Unit in Edinburgh (Evans, 1982). This young psychiatrist—and author of this introduction—had been allocated the prime task of engaging half of the sixteen young men and women (between the ages of 15 and 20 years), resident in the unit, in psychoanalytically orientated group psychotherapy. The role of group therapist demanded great discipline and was limited to interpretations about the meaning for the group as a whole of the discussions and other contributions generated by the young people (Ezriel, 1950; Sutherland, 1965). This role was made more taxing by the fact that most of the discussion was about the failings of the "group therapist", the failings of the unit as a whole, and "concern" to "help" the hapless therapist out of his "absurd" role by inviting him to participate directly in the activities "preferred" by the members of the group—which would include tasting various pleasures based on sex, drugs, and possibly a little violence in order to keep fit. This "innocent" young psychiatrist could have easily dismissed all these taunts as "resistance" had it not been for the fact that there was one exception to this litany of derision of the therapeutic services with which these young people had been provided. One of the conditions of admission of a young person to the unit—and these people came with a wide range of problem definitions, from various forms of psychosis to delinquent personality, and from all over Scotland—was that both (if there were two) parents were required to attend a weekly multi-family therapy group with their own young person together with half of the other young people in the unit and their attached parents—in fact, all the young people who attended my daily therapy group.

Those multi-family therapy groups, where they had to face their parents as well as the parents of the young people they were actually living with—what one might guess would be a "nightmare scenario" for many young people—were the *only* therapeutic experience that they thought—or at least said they thought—had any value at all. I say *those* groups because they were off limits to us young psychiatrists. They were run by the nursing staff and were supervised by the Director of the unit without our participation (Harrow, 1970). So it made me think. Perhaps there was something that these young people were seeing that some of us had missed or not properly understood.

The second story is shorter: it is more of a reminiscence about the thinking we encountered in the "depths"—both literally and metaphorically—of the Marlborough Day Hospital. The clinic contained what was described as a "water room", which in turn was perceived as the core of the treatment of children admitted to the hospital's Autistic Unit. Many might question the appropriateness of the diagnosis of autism appended to some of the children who attended there, but the thinking about the treatment was clear: that the problems the children encountered were safely inside them, and that they could therefore appropriately be the passive recipients of a "cure"—in this case, based on "water-play" work. Reflecting about it later, it seemed close to that cure loved by the gentility of the nineteenth century, known as the spa: a place where the "waters" would hopefully cleanse and wash away the "badness" contained in the individual. In fact the search for individual explanations of "deficit" was probably an efficient nineteenth-century ploy to avoid facing the increasing evidence of mutual and collective responsibility for social deviance and poverty, a ploy that may have been felt as essential if the artificially preserved differences between people of economics, class, and later ethnicity were to be maintained. Observation of this unit suggested not only that it was an anachronism—a hangover from such thinking—and that many of the children would not have been accepted within Kanner's (1943) or even later definitions of autism, but it also patently failed to meet the local needs for families and children in "trouble". So when we reviewed the goals and function of this unit, we found ourselves asking the question—not what is the most severe disorder of children, but who are the children and their families who the most seem to fall foul of the social, medical, and educational services. In fact, the weight of the case notes became a more valid tool in making the diagnosis than did the individual quirks of any one particular child in a family. It was this idea—that the amount of professional scrutiny or writing about a family might be in inverse relationship to the benefit that the family derived from "using" the different services—that led us to ask our managers and funders from the different agencies to allow us to use the resources for what the authors later define in this book as "multi-problem", or "*multi-professional*", families.

As psychotherapy, counselling, and related personal services have developed throughout Europe—some would say "mushroomed"—so the focus on listening to the individual's "inner account" has increasingly dominated the "non-medical" aspects of mental health thinking. But as anyone who has lived in a family knows only too well, life cannot necessarily be constructed on the basis of each person's individual inner needs. If conceived in that way, then those needs—between different adults or different children as well as between the adults and the children—often conflict. Child protection, in particular, has to focus on family relationships and on how these can be constructed in such a way that children experience sufficient safety as well as nurture and that the adults have sufficient understanding of each other's predicaments that they can achieve a lasting and workable compromise. The very process of creating a multi-family group is an intervention that invites that process; it is a structural intervention (Minuchin, 1974; Minuchin & Fishman, 1981) in that it can demonstrate that in a *different* context people *can* choose to behave *differently* with each other and can find different ways of seeing, thinking about, and reacting to each other in the various life situations in which previously conflict had seemed inevitable.

The third story is the briefest. When we first set up multi-family groups in what became the Family Day Unit, we had no idea what to do. We had all come from psychoanalytic backgrounds, so what we knew about was making interpretations of behaviour—just as I had been expected to do with those perceptive adolescents described above. So, with seven or eight families in a room, they began to talk, play, or fight, or all three and more at once. We made comments—comments about the common themes in what they said and did, comments that suggested explanations, or at least meanings, of particular behaviours. And there was consternation. Parents objected to the apparent slurs on their persons. Children became so excited that we had to rescue some from the top of a high garden wall, and some from the roof of a three-storey building. This was the beginning of the learning that Asen, Dawson, and McHugh elucidate so clearly in the rest of this book. But even then we had already learnt some positive lessons. The role of being a *parent* in a multi-family context seemed to allow some self-respect, and for some participants it counteracted what they had experienced as the demeaning experience of being a *patient* in the mental health services. As one young mother who had had a number of hospital admissions for alcohol-related psychiatric disorders put it: "Here I'm Lucy's mum. . . . I'm being helped to maintain my care of her, but I know I care and the others can see that. As a *patient*, nobody thought about who I could care about. "

But this is a book about the power of changing contexts and about the freedom that even those caught in the deprived, as well as vindictive, spirals can sometimes make when the context is organized in such a way that it faces them with new options. The 1960s was a time of much scrutiny of the roles played by psychiatrists and related mental health professionals in people's lives. In the United Kingdom, the writings of Laing, Cooper, and others (e.g. Laing, 1960) focused on the power invested in a professional with the right to define another's sanity and also challenged both the practices as well as the fundamental tenets of the profession of psychiatry—creating what later became known as the anti-psychiatry movement. While the authors of this book might be sympathetic to some of the critiques of the mental health services as they were at that time, these critiques still focused on the patient and his or her "world view".

Even the family explorations of Laing and Esterson (1964) were in general limited to providing insights into what may have made the patient's life "untenable". Goffman (1961) had shown in his compelling writings the power that institutions had to define their inmates in negative frames of reference, and in turn the power that these could have on how an individual both behaved and defined him/herself. In the present book, Asen discusses the implied contradiction contained in the title of one publication about institutional development: "An Institution for Change" (Cooklin, Miller, & McHugh, 1983). The anti-psychiatry movement of the 1960s, however, had minimal impact on the shape and operation of actual mental health services. As the family therapy movement began to influence the United Kingdom, so attempts were made to widen this perspective, but attracting the often-valid criticism that the "internal pathology" of the patient was simply replaced with the "pathology" of the family. This criticism applied to work in both child as well as adult mental health.

The development of the Marlborough Family Service probably fell into all the above traps. In particular it became an "Institution" for family therapy. However, two common aspects of "institutionalization"—the perception of all aspects of the institution and its activities as the inmate's primary reference point (what the canteen server said this morning being more important than a national crisis!) and an assumption that all the professionals both inside and outside the institution share all knowledge about oneself—were challenged by the very structure of this unit. Fortunately, it also attracted criticism from the local community about the "rigidity" of its practices, and, even more fortunately, the staff team of the Marlborough listened and began to make a different response. What is described in this book is part of that different response. We had already moved from the patient to the family, and then from the family to the community, but the "community" as an entity

posed problems. The concept of a "society" was being scorned by
our then Conservative government—particularly by its leader,
Margaret Thatcher—and the concept of "community" seemed
about to follow suite. At the same time, the word "community"
was in universal use in both the media as well as NHS management documents, for all things from the "Community Charge"—a
most unpopular local tax—to the "ethnic-minority community"—
which almost certainly did not exist as any form of community. So
what the Marlborough team set up was an explicitly artificial community of families—a new social context which they hoped could
provide different experiences, and encourage new pathways of
living, for families who often saw themselves as at "the bottom of
the pile".

This book describes the success of that venture and the various
multi-family approaches that have developed from it. So why is
the basic approach still relatively so rare? As the authors point out
in this book, some have used the approach, but only as specific
interventions for specific populations with particular problems. As
they also point out, common explanations of the relative lack of
multi-family work are given as:

1. lack of resources such as adequate rooms, staff, and so forth;
2. lack of skills;
3. problems in the recruiting of families.

The Marlborough team were fortunate in having suitable
rooms and interested staff. As more families were referred from
the courts, the team also had an increasingly "captive audience" of
families. As my third story suggests, initially we had little skill.
The "shocking" experience suggested in that story probably meant
we learnt fast by trial and error, and, as Asen describes, we made
use of many opportunities for help in developing our skills: from
Minuchin, the "Milan" team, and others.

Therefore, overcoming the resistance to "creating" multi-family groups probably needs to be seen in a broader professional
context. It constitutes a move outside the defined roles of mental
health staff. Even in "stranger-group" therapy, it may be a moot
point whether the therapist actually fulfils a significant function in

comparison with the effect of the group as a whole. If not, then the therapist is essentially a "convenor"—someone who brings the group together and provides it with its *raison d'être*. However, in such groups the role of the therapist is at least reasonably well-defined. As Asen points out, a strength in multi-family groups results from the frequent changes in role which the staff may adopt, and in these groups it is even more apparent that the power of the group as a therapeutic agent significantly eclipses anything that the therapist, or even therapists, do. Increasingly the role becomes a combination of convenor and "stage manager" of the event. In practice, this does require considerable skill, as well as considerable knowledge about both the disorders under discussion and the factors that allow families to develop strength and resilience. But it is a less visible role in the face of the powerful and compelling experiences manifested by the participants. Overcoming one's timidity about this experimentation with the professional's role, as well as confronting the practical details of convening such an event, are probably the key obstacles to setting up what are increasingly being recognized as highly therapeutic "contexts".

As Asen, McHugh, and Dawson demonstrate in this book, their work rewrites in part their own professional histories as well as those of the families who participate. The rapid and frequent changes in context which they describe include many different sets of relationships between parents and children, spouses, children and other children, adults and other adults, adults and staff, and so on. By definition, these changes also represent changes for the staff—at one moment acting as a therapist for one family, at another one of a group of therapists for a multi-family group, participating in a shopping expedition or as a "partner" in the preparation of a meal. While this mobility in the roles of the staff members both mirrors and complements the many changes experienced by the participants, in the "tight" programme described by the authors it also sets an example of flexibility, as well as providing the staff with many different vantage points from which to intervene. The use of "cross-family" or surrogate family relationships as a therapeutic tool, as well as the setting of reciprocal goals for the adults by the children—as the authors describe—can be seen to follow logically from that thinking. The contexts in which they work, as described throughout the book, are "high risk" for the families referred to them. They do not talk of inter-family dia-logues in a way that presents either false modesty or any sugges-tion that "dialogues" are all that these families need. However, the book is a powerful invitation to colleagues to follow the authors' example in taking valuable risks and, in particular, to experiment with the new professional roles offered by the experience of work-ing in multi-family group contexts.

Alan Cooklin
London

MULTIPLE FAMILY
THERAPY

CHAPTER ONE

Developing a contextual approach

The work described in this book has been developed over the past twenty-five years at the Marlborough Family Service. This is a publicly funded institution, part of Britain's National Health Service, serving a defined catchment area and located in the middle of London. The Marlborough offers a range of therapeutic and consultative work for children, teenagers, adults, couples, and families. It is a child and family consultation service, integrated with the adult psychotherapy service and with a strong link to the local community health team which caters for seriously mentally ill adults. The Marlborough is an all-age service, with the youngest client 2 days of age and the oldest 96 years old. It therefore can take referrals without having to be limited by the traditionally rigid age boundaries between child and adolescent and adult and old-age mental heath services. The Marlborough is staffed by a multidisciplinary team of child, adult, and family therapists, social workers, teachers, nurses, clinical psychologist, and psychiatrists. All staff, however diverse their trainings and interests, share the basic values of the family systems approach. This means adopting an interactional framework that counteracts

1

the potential for overemphasizing individual blame. Conceptualizing behaviour in the context of relationships is liberating as it offers the potential for a far-wider range of choices about how things might change if they have got stuck. The approach developed—the Marlborough model—above all emphasizes context: individuals live in contexts, usually families. Families live in contexts: their neighbourhoods. Within their living context, families and their individual members relate to friendship networks, to work spheres, to schools or nurseries, to religious or cultural institutions, to professional networks which enter their lives. A contextual approach attempts to address all these contexts, all the different systems and sub-systems of which the child, the adult, and the family are part.

Twenty-five years ago this emphasis on context seemed somewhat out of place. The biomedical model, then as dominant as it is now, looks for causes of disorder inside the person, inside the person's mind and brain. The preferred site of intervention is the individual or part of the individual. In this model, relatively little importance is attributed to context or to interpersonal issues, with funding mostly going to research into genes and biochemistry. While this approach has some merit, when working with disadvantaged individuals and families it can prove unrewarding. Their daily suffering—from poverty to racism, from poor education to other forms of discrimination and social exclusion, from their daily struggles with alcohol abuse to intra-familial violence—is so predominant that any interventions have to have a large psychosocial dimension. It is simply not possible to focus on neurones when the larger system hurts.

When Dr Alan Cooklin became the director of the Marlborough in 1976, the institution was known as the Marlborough Day Hospital, clearly signalling a medical framework with all its implications of "patients", "illness", and "treatment". One of Alan Cooklin's first actions was to change the name to the Marlborough Family Service, reflecting its new emphasis: providing a service to families. Initially, many referrers were more than puzzled by this sudden re-naming and re-framing. They found it difficult to know how to refer families when, in their view, it was the individual who had problems or was ill. However, undeterred by these initial responses, the Marlborough team embarked on a course of educating referrers. These told us that they simply did not know how to tell one of their clients or patients that they should have "family therapy". They were worried that they might alienate them. All they wanted was to send a difficult problem to the Marlborough and leave it to us to sort it out, with or without the family. We gradually accepted that it was our job—and not that of the referrer—to turn individuals into families. This meant frequently that the referred person was seen on his or her own, but individual sessions were conducted in such a way that therapeutic system was kept open, ready for family members to join as soon as possible (Jenkins & Asen, 1992).

Desperate to practise "family therapy" in the late 1970s, we subjected each and every referral to this mode of treatment. Having encountered the great family therapy stars, including Minuchin, Haley, Watzlawick, Palazzoli, and Ackerman, we treated families between once weekly and once monthly with our peculiar brand of family therapy. We discovered soon that while our approach seemed to work for some families, it did not for others. Once-weekly or once-fortnightly family therapy certainly did not seem intensive enough for some of the types of families that were increasingly referred to us. These families seemed to have many different problems simultaneously, with seemingly chaotic structures, diffuse or non-existent boundaries between various sub-systems, high degrees of enmeshment, and the absence of hierarchies. One very striking feature was that these families presented themselves as united in relation to the outside world (and social services/social welfare departments in particular), while at the same time failing to organize internal family affairs, such as finances, household work, child care, employment, and day-to-day activities. It was our encounters with the seemingly disorganized families that first led us to pose a crucial question which remains a guiding principle for much of our work: "What is the context that we need to use or invent in order to address the issues that this family or this referrer wants or needs to address?" Weekly family therapy seemed entirely insufficient to address the multiple issues in these families, which often included violence, drug or alcohol abuse, adult mental illness, social exclusion, and other daunting presentations. We therefore had the idea of creating a day unit that families could attend six to eight hours a day every day of the week for weeks or months. It also seemed to us that having quite a number of families attending at the same time might help deal with their social exclusion and isolation. Problems such as physical and sexual abuse, alcoholism, and domestic violence have a tendency to isolate families from neighbours and friends (Asen, George, Piper, & Stevens, 1989). Moreover, the stigma attached to these problems further enhances the sense of being different or feeling marginalized. Bringing families together and encouraging them to make contact with one another counteracts such isolation. The Family Day Unit was thus born (see chapter two).

Through our work with seemingly chaotic families, who often did not come to appointments and therefore had to be seen at least initially in their homes, we have never really been able to avoid seeing and experiencing their contexts. This has meant seeing the problems where they manifest themselves. Undertaking outreach work implied encountering families in contexts that are quite different from traditional clinic settings, with their one-way mirrors, videotape, and teams of fours. No such luxuries were or are available when working with families in their homes.

The Marlborough Family Service receives each week between ten and twenty new referrals, from a whole range of different sources, such as doctors, social workers, schools and courts, as well as self-referrals. The team meets at the beginning of each week and considers how to respond to these different requests. The principle that guides the work is embodied in the question: "What is the most relevant context within which to respond to the request?" This question frames the possible response. For example, it is possible to think that it might be best for the referred person to be seen on her or his own. It is also possible to consider that it might be more relevant for the person to be seen together with one other significant person, or the whole family. It is also possible to consider seeing the referred person together with the referrer and members of the family. Or, a meeting with the referrer only might be regarded as the most appropriate way to address the presenting problem. And there are other possibilities. In other words, when it comes to choosing the "relevant context" there is a whole range of options, and the clinician will have to reflect on which of these should be pursued, based on the information provided, on the clinician's prejudices—and on a number of other factors. The place where the first and subsequent encounters take place is another context: it could be the home, a school, a family day unit, a mental hospital, an office. Many different responses are possible to each individual request for help or consultation. If therapists continually question their own practices, uncomfortable though this may be at times, then they are more likely to ensure that they provide appropriate contexts for therapy, rather than fitting clients and their families into institutional contexts. Our own team has critically examined our practices on many occasions. For example, at one time we thought that we could best deal with all clients and their problems referred to us by reframing these as soon as possible into family issues. Logically, we prescribed family therapy which was dished out by a therapist, with colleagues behind a one-way screen, preferably in teams of four, and sessions lasting for 60–90 minutes. While this context is still relevant for some clients, we no longer believe that everyone benefits from it or that it is indeed appropriate in many cases.

The search some eighteen years ago for relevant contexts for change led us to invent a family school (see chapter three). This was in response to being asked to provide services for pupils who had been excluded from their schools because of serious learning difficulties, violence, or disruptive behaviours. The schools seemed to lay all the blame at the family's door, while the family tended to blame the school entirely for the educational failure of the children. The more the family blamed the school, the more the school blamed the family. Soon an impasse was reached, with the child caught between the warring parties. The family refused to seek psychiatric or psychological help, and the teachers no longer wanted these difficult children in their classes. To overcome this impasse, we decided to open a "family school", where parents could witness their children's educational problems and where teachers could witness the family issues that are often transferred into school. The focus for intervention was not on the individual pupil, but on the whole family and the school system. Designing a model of therapeutic practice set in a classroom proved to be effective in creating situations and opportunities for interventions with children and their parents. The unique feature of the Marlborough

Family School is that all children who attend have to be accompanied by at least one parent, thus creating a unique context for change.

Another observation we made, when looking at referral patterns, was that we had remarkably few clients and families from the different minority ethnic cultures that are so prevalent in the centre of London, with its huge first- and second-generation immigrant population. We had to ask ourselves what it was that made it so difficult for families from other cultures to access our services. Posing the question "What is the context that we need to create to get these families to use our service?" again proved useful. We examined our own practices, including our own prejudices and non-conscious racist practices. We started recruiting colleagues from different cultures, and we talked to community leaders. Eventually we managed to persuade local politicians and health managers to fund a programme by which we would employ and train community workers from Bangladesh, India, Pakistan, and China in delivering culture-appropriate systemic services to their local communities. Of course, this had to be a two-way process: these colleagues also had to train the Marlborough team to understand their cultures and the specific meanings of symptoms and illnesses within these. Five years ago, our Asian Counselling Service was born and now receives many referrals particularly from the Bangladeshi community. Chinese clients and their families have proved more difficult to engage, and, again, we asked ourselves "What is the relevant context that we need to create or utilize for us to be able to provide relevant services for this population?" This led us to set up an outreach project in Soho—London's Chinatown—where once a week, in a Chinese health centre, two of our Chinese family counsellors see people on "site", which is much more acceptable in the local community than being seen out of their familiar context.

The Marlborough Family Service, with its clinicians, has over the years undergone considerable changes, some of them less comfortable than others. It has invented, discarded, and re-invented therapeutic contexts for change and in this way attempted to provide relevant contexts for change for many clients, their families, and intervening professionals. Given that it often seems arbitrary as to who the identified patient or designated client is, the

Marlborough has adopted an all-age referral policy, thus bridging the often unhelpful gap between child- and adult-oriented mental health services. This has allowed us to work with anybody who is sent for help—irrespective of their age or presenting problem. These seemingly ill- or undefined entry criteria to our service have resulted in us receiving a vast range of clients and problems, often those that no other agency wanted to deal with. The impetus for starting multiple family group work was very much related to one specific client group: those families that had more than their fair share of difficulties.

Multi-problem families

The term "multi-problem families" is quite problematic and has very different meanings to professionals, lay persons, and indeed the families who are so labelled. Clearly, it is a potentially stigmatizing description, one that many of the families themselves would not accept. Clinicians tend to use this term as shorthand for a number of characteristics that seem common to certain families. Some of these are referred to as "treatment-resistant" or "intractable" families, terms that surely should not have a place in a circular model, as they suggest a linear relationship between persons who provide treatment and other persons who accept, resist, or reject such treatment. Implied in the term "treatment resistant" is the reproachful question that asks how these families dare to defeat the well-meaning efforts of therapists to make them "get better". The interactional nature of the concept of "treatment resistance" is made apparent by posing specific reflexive questions. For example:

1. "What is it that this family does that makes me believe that they are intractable?"
2. "What is it that I do as a therapist that makes the family behave as if they were intractable?"

This type of curious inquiry challenges the seeming intractability of certain families, a point so well made in the original Milan team's descriptions of the paradoxical relationships that their client families had with helpers (Selvini Palazzoli, Boscolo, Cecchin, & Prata, 1980).

A "typical" feature of so-called multi-problem families is their apparent "chaotic" structure (Minuchin et al., 1967), with diffuse or non-existent boundaries between various sub-systems, high degrees of enmeshment, and an absence of hierarchies. As stated earlier in this chapter, these families frequently present themselves as united in relation to the outside world but at the same time fail to organize their internal family affairs (Asen et al., 1982). This apparent lack of structure evokes the wish in professionals to create a context that is very structured. The initial design of the Marlborough Family Day Unit programme very much reflected this—a tightly constructed timetable requiring families constantly to adapt to the ever-changing contexts and requirements.

Violence is another common feature in these families: violence between partners, violence of parent against child, violence of child against parent, violence between children, violence of parents against professionals—and, from the families' point of view, violence of professionals against families. The language of violence, both physical and verbal, evokes strong responses from professionals who not infrequently react by being (socially) violent themselves, acting in punitive ways through removal of a child or adult via Emergency Protections Orders, Care Orders, or Sectioning under the Mental Health Act. On other occasions, the responses of professionals can be seen as being violent by omission—for example, when little or no protection is offered to children who are known to be the victims of domestic violence. In such circumstances, the professional network itself can become "dangerous" (Dale, 1986). Moreover, professionals tend to defend themselves against their own anxieties by involving an ever-increasing number of colleagues. This does precious little as far as clarity and focus are concerned and usually results in fragmentation and confusion, rendering already vulnerable children and adults even more vulnerable. Such fragmentation of helping responses and potential splits within the helping system can be addressed when families attend a multiple family therapy programme, where they are seen for a significant time each day. This alone gives a strong message to the network and relieves anxieties temporarily. Once the families and professional system have agreed to such intensive work, the risk of uncoordinated offers of "help" is significantly reduced. In a day-unit setting, families often feel initially as if they are being put under a microscope. This inevitably puts pressure on them, leading to tension and crises as well as to mutual learning. In our programme, any such crises are controlled as they take place in a therapeutic environment, under the eyes of many people, both staff and clients.

Far from providing a sanctuary from everyday stresses, multi-family settings are expressly intended to create and replicate familiar crises. Having a number of families present at the same time intensifies living. Providing a therapeutic context that deliberately generates crises (Minuchin, 1974)—crises that are familiar in that they revolve around everyday issues—allows planning and a proactive approach. However, this is very different from the apparently random production of crises that multi-problem families tend to achieve, forcing professionals continually to react. Deliberately creating contexts that are intensive allows exploration of and experimentation with different behaviours, whether this is around issues of violence, inappropriate sexual behaviours, or drug and alcohol abuse.

Another feature commonly present in so-called multi-problem families is their sense of social isolation. The stigma of mental illness, of abuse, or of violence is addressed when different families presenting with similar problems of living exchange their experiences and can feel that they are "all in the same boat".

It is extremely rare for middle-class families to acquire the label "multi-problem family". There is a strong social dimension to this concept: multi-problem families tend to be at the bottom of the class system and to be socially disadvantaged. They tend to consist of unemployed, single parents with multiple short-term relationships; adults and children who have daily experiences of racial abuse and discrimination; or people who live below the poverty line, frequently in appalling housing conditions. Many multi-problem families seem stuck in their habitual ways of interacting with one another around child-care tasks, play, outings, or relationship issues. Exploring these in a group setting can feel liberating, particularly if group tasks are set that inspire playfulness. Chronic relationships with helpers have been described above. The intensity of these relationships gets diluted when families attend a multiple family group. With only very few staff available, the focus is shifted onto other families.

In summary, specifically designed units that specialize in multiple family therapy and run whole-day programmes over prolonged periods of time will tend to target a very chronic population of individuals and their families. Such intensive input can be justified by pointing to the huge amount of resources being poured into these families by health, social services, and education officials. The provision of day units for multi-problem and multi-agency families is cost-effective, makes a lot of real difference, and often mobilizes families that have been written off by the system.

CHAPTER TWO

Multiple family therapy—history and concepts

The idea of treating a number of families together was first pioneered in the early 1960s by Laqueur and his co-workers (Laqueur, La Burt, & Morong, 1964). This group saw the multi-family setting as a useful context for trying out different behaviours and new role relationships. Here, the resources of all family members could be used more successfully, with several families being treated together in one group. The major aims was to improve inter- and intra-family communication, in the hope that this might help relatives to understand some of the troubled behaviours of the index patient. This led to running groups for schizophrenics and their relatives (Laqueur, 1972). Laqueur worked initially with schizophrenic patients and their families on a hospital ward—alongside insulin-shock treatment. He saw this as a pragmatic response to the need for improving ward management.

At the outset, multiple family therapy was a rather peculiar blend of group therapy and family therapy, introduced at a time of dwindling inpatient resources. Laqueur and his team worked from the premise that difficulties in relationships derive from dysfunctional feedback loops across subsystem boundaries. However, he also made use of other theoretical models, such as psychodynamic ideas and attachment theory. He hypothesized that in normal development secondary objects of attachment gradually replace primary ones and that therefore the presence of other families allowed a person to struggle towards increasing independence and self-differentiation by identifying with members of other families and learning by analogy (Laqueur, 1973).

The early multi-family groups were appropriately described as a "sheltered workshop in family communication" (Laqueur et al., 1964). By working with four or five families at a time, Laqueur witnessed "improved" communications and "better" understanding in these families as they learnt directly and indirectly from each other. He also observed that, as a therapist, he felt less constrained than when just one family was continuously the sole focus of the work.

Bateson's idea of describing problems in behaviour as restraints of redundancy and restraints of feedback seemed relevant in this context (Bateson, 1973). Restraints of redundancy refers to people's restricted internal world views; restraints of feedback refers to the pattern of interaction between people and the circular feedback of events whereby people become restrained within the dominant story. Within this framework, the multi-family paradigm offers multiple perspectives through double description: when there is more than one description, a second or third is introduced which can trigger the reception of new information.

Laqueur's early work inspired many different clinicians. McFarlane developed a multi-family therapy programme in a psychiatric hospital (McFarlane, 1982). He saw the following as the main ingredients of this approach: resocialization, stigma reversal, modulated dis-enmeshment, communication normalization, and crisis management. McFarlane observed that "insight" by the family or its individual members was not essential for therapeutic change. Instead, he believed that families might see a bit of themselves in others, including their own "dysfunctions"—and that this produced learning without there being a need for it to be made explicit.

Anderson (1983) developed a psycho-educational approach with multi-family groups. Her model argues that meaning and understanding evolve through the dynamic social process of dialogue and conversation, given that it is through language that we are able to maintain meaningful human contact with each other and that it is language through which we share a reality. Anderson's descriptions as to the use and effectiveness of the multi-family model are in many ways similar to McFarlane's. Anderson saw the aims of psycho-educational multi-family work with families of schizophrenics as helping them to expand their social network and to reduce stigma, relieving the carer burden, reducing Expressed Emotion in key relatives, and facilitating more tolerance as far as the family's attitude in relation to the ill person is concerned. She argued that, by alleviating communication deviance, more functional communication patterns could emerge. It was Anderson's view that, by offering family support, a bridge would be formed between families and psychiatric contexts.

At that time, it seemed that multiple family work was most appropriate for families with limited social contacts (Leichter & Schulman, 1974; McFarlane, 1993), providing them with the opportunity to discuss common issues and to give and receive emotional support. Unlike traditional psychodynamic group therapy, families participating in multiple family therapy group work were encouraged to socialize outside the group setting. McFarlane (1982) states unequivocally that it is a sign that the group and individuals have developed when families socialize outside the "therapeutic" setting.

The multiple family therapy model has been further elaborated over the past three decades and applied to various psychiatric populations, notably psychotics (Anderson, 1983; Lansky, 1981; McFarlane, 1982; Strelnick, 1977). It is interesting to note that multiple family therapy was usually not given as a sole treatment in its own right, but in addition to other concurrent treatments (Reiss & Costell, 1977). By the end of the twentieth century, it was and still is now a well-established ingredient in the work with schizophrenic patients (Kuipers, Leff, & Lam, 1992). Multiple family therapy is also now practised in many other presentations and conditions (O'Shea & Phelps, 1985), including drug and alcohol abuse (Kaufman & Kaufman, 1979), chronic medical illness (Gonsalez, Steinglass, & Reiss, 1989), Huntingdon's disease (Murburg, Price, & Jalali, 1988), child abuse (Asen et al., 1989), eating disorders (Slagerman & Yager, 1989) and more specifically bulimia nervosa (Wooley & Lewis, 1987), and a mixture of in- and outpatient children and adolescents presenting with a variety of problems (Wattie, 1994).

It is evident from this account that over the years practitioners, in different parts of Europe and the United States, have generated projects involving the simultaneous therapeutic involvement of families. These tended to be based around specific problem areas and presentations, often created *ad hoc* and therefore having a limited life-span. To our knowledge the Marlborough Family Day Unit in London was the first institution providing a permanent multi-family setting, specifically designed for and solely dedicated to such work. Over the years, similar family day units as well as some residential family units, based on the Marlborough model, have been established outside Britain—for example, in Scandinavia, the Netherlands, Germany, and Italy. While their work has been informed by some of our practices, the ideas have often been creatively transformed and been adapted to the specific cultural and work contexts. Reference will be made to some of these European projects in the relevant chapters of this book.

The Marlborough Family Service pioneered a unique approach in the late 1970s (Asen et al., 1982; Cooklin, 1982; Cooklin et al., 1983), creating a day hospital where up to ten families would attend together for five days a week for eight hours a day. The clients targeted were so-called multi-problem families, with more than one member presenting with psychiatric or antisocial symptoms and problems. Here the main mode of treatment was multi-family work, with other forms of treatment used only occasionally. Such work in a multi-family milieu is essentially different from multi-family therapy carried out in outpatient settings in addition to other forms of ongoing treatment. The underlying concepts of and reasons for multiple family therapy are shown in Table 2.1.

Families containing a problematic individual frequently experience a strong sense of *social isolation*. Even close friends are no longer invited for meals or other social occasions, because of intense feelings of shame and guilt. Going out in public as a family with an obviously disturbed family member can be very embarrassing. Meeting with other families who experience similar diffi-

Table 2.1:   Reasons for Multiple Family Therapy

Overcoming social isolation

Expansion of social network

Overcoming stigmatization

Creating solidarity

Creating new and multiple perspectives

Learning from each other

Providing mutual support and feedback

Encouraging active parental involvement

Neutralizing chronic staff–patient relationships

Experimenting with surrogate parenting

Creating hot-house effects

Injecting hope

culties allows for these to be shared, creating a mutual feeling that "we are all in the same boat".

By mixing for large parts of the day with other families and engaging interactively, there is soon an *expansion of the social network*—clearly an advantage to families who are usually socially isolated. Many of the families form friendships that often continue long after the therapeutic work has finished.

This interaction can have strong *de-stigmatizing* effects: in multi-family settings, such families are not outsiders but are in the majority. Moreover, the presence of only relatively few professional staff contributes to a "family" rather than "medical" atmosphere.

This also results in people not feeling so central, as they are part of a large group and the feeling of being constantly watched and observed by staff is less intense and thus less persecutory. Feelings of being watched and judged are not at all uncommon: almost all parents experience intense guilt and self-doubt. To see other parents struggling with similar feelings creates a sense of *solidarity* and reduces some of the burden experienced by the carers.

However, being in the presence of other families highlights not only similarities but also differences. Families cannot help becoming curious about one another, and this results in them viewing their predicaments *from new and multiple perspectives*. In a multi-family setting, there are many possible ways of viewing things. Eating-disordered families, for example, tend to have distorted self-perceptions while being often very precise and intuitive about other families.

This is of considerable therapeutic use not only to the families themselves but also to other families attending at the same time. It allows parents and adolescents to *learn from each other*. If therapists encourage feedback between families, then this can lead to mutual learning. The therapeutic team's continuous encouragement of families to respond to one another and to comment on their obser-vations—not only of themselves but also of other families—creates a context for mutual reflection and a seemingly endless set of potential feedback loops.

Peer support and peer criticism are known to be powerful dy-namics that can promote change. Many people find it easier to use *mutual support and feedback* from fellow-sufferers than from staff—it seems more "credible" because these families all have painful direct experiences of similar issues. Such feedback gets generated during a whole range of different activities throughout the day, from joint meals, informal encounters, formal large-group discus-sions, creative art work, or outings.

In this way, there is *active parental involvement* in the treatment and management of their children—and vice versa. This is very different from the experiences on hospital wards, where relatives are usually reduced to passive onlookers while the medical team gets on with the treatment. In a multi-family setting, with very few staff present, families get the constant message that it is *their* job to deal with the problems and related issues.

Such parental involvement can also be helpful to staff in that it can defuse or *neutralize chronic staff–patient relationships*. The battles that many chronic patients are involved in for months when ad-mitted to inpatient units often result in staff getting drawn in and behaving in complementary ways which can be anti-therapeutic. Putting such "professional" patients into a multi-family context immediately puts them on a spot: they can be challenged by fellow patients and families. Staff are no longer the primary reference-point for patients, as they so often seem to be in institutions, with an underlying assumption that they have total knowledge. The boundaries that families and their members have to develop in relation to one another are very different from those based on opposition to professionals or agencies. This can have positive effects on staff, who soon realize that difficult patients involve themselves in identical battles with their own and other families. Such recognition frequently has the effect of improving relationships between staff and patient, with staff feeling less personally persecuted.

Another therapeutic potential of multi-family work lies in the possibility of experimenting with *surrogate parenting*. Actively encouraging the parents of one child to act as surrogates to the child of other parents (and vice versa) may not only provide a parent used to being seen as a "failure" with some success, but can also change the perception of a "problem" and how this may differ in another context. Dealing, for short and well-defined periods, with the child of another family (or, conversely, with another parent), "crossing over" as it were, may allow new experiences to take place. A depressed teenager, for example, is likely to have different interactions with the mother of a fellow sufferer from those with her own mother. Moreover, this mother may find it easier to have a conversation about a contentious issue with this girl than she would with her own daughter. Such an experience, witnessed not only by the two persons interacting but also by the "other" mother and daughter, tends to stimulate useful reflections about how things might be able to develop differently.

Bringing a whole number of families together for intensive days or weeks creates a *hot-house effect*. Interactions are necessarily more intense in a group setting where children and parents are participating in different tasks and where they are required to examine not only their own but also other families' communications and behaviours. This increased intensity can lead to rapid growth—change is more likely to take place, as familiar coping and defence mechanisms cannot be employed. Being part of a multi-family setting requires families constantly to change context, requiring each family member continually having to adapt to new demands. Such intensity cannot easily be created in individual family sessions.

The sheer energy released in the course of such a programme provides a new structure for children, adolescents, and parents alike and *injects hope*. Such feelings of hope can be enhanced by mixing families who have gone through a multi-family programme with others who are new to it. It is a common experience that parents who have benefited from being part of such a programme and whose children have made good progress are much better at explaining these benefits than any of the staff ever could. When "old" families tell their story, this is frequently a considerable source of encouragement for the "new" parents, with a kind of preview of changes that might be possible for their offspring and for themselves.

CHAPTER THREE

Developing a day unit for families

*From individual group therapy
to family group therapy*

This chapter describes the history and past and present work of the Marlborough Family Day Unit—probably the first of its kind in the world. In a paper entitled "An Institution for Change: Developing a Family Day Unit", Alan Cooklin, the founder of the Marlborough Family Day Unit, provocatively juxtaposes the concepts of "change" and "institution" (Cooklin et al., 1983). The notion of institutionalized change seems full of contradictions, and it was the encounter with many seemingly "impossible" families that generated the idea of creating an institution specializing in promoting change for these families.

The idea of bringing together so-called multi-problem families for joint therapy was inspired by the therapeutic community movement, believing—as it did at the time—in ideas such as "democracy", "openness", and "shared responsibility". Maxwell Jones (1968) had experimented with the creation of a "social" therapy, involving adults who had been invariably diagnosed as suffering from personality disorder or psychopathy. He believed that, by putting them together in a "real living situation" in a therapeutic milieu, they might dilute the traditional mental hospital setting and de-medicalize their own treatment. This ethos reflected a move away from traditional authoritarian hospital hierarchies to a setting where patients—nowadays called "users"—would not only participate in their own treatment, but also be involved in helping fellow sufferers. The idea of having the potential to be helpful, rather than being simply at the receiving end of some help, seemed a first step to decrease the dependence of chronic patients on institutions and to mobilize self-help resources. Jones's model seemed to make sense for groups of individuals, and if it worked— might it not work for groups of families?

The reason for designing the Family Day Unit was inspired by the recognition that certain families seemed very expert at attracting increasing numbers of professionals (56 in one celebrated case) while at the same time not making any effective use of the various medical, psychiatric, social, and educational resources offered. Such "multi-agency" families proved notoriously difficult to manage, as some or many individual members were treated by different agencies and professionals, often over many years, but with little coordination between the different services. Inviting these families for weekly family therapy sessions seemed at best like a drop in the ocean and, at worst, like only the addition of yet another agency, destined to increase the confusion of who was doing what to whom for what purpose. Any therapeutic ventures tended to be accompanied by removal of a child into care, repeated hospital admissions of an adult, exclusion from school, and other social-control types of interventions. This rendered therapy virtually ineffective. To overcome this impasse, Alan Cooklin and his team had the idea, back in 1976, to put a number of these families together under one roof for prolonged periods of time, in the hope of somehow breaking the cycle of repeated crises that resulted in fragmentation of help offered.

Phases of the evolution of the Family Day Unit

The Family Day Unit has gone through a number of phases over the past two decades and this section describes its development, highlighting how different systemic ideas and evolving personal and political contexts have resulted in institutional changes and practices.

Phase 1:   Therapeutic community phase

The main guiding idea for setting up a day unit for families was to bring together many different facets of life in a therapeutic milieu. At the time, much of it was inspired by psychoanalytic notions of the institution and its staff acting as a kind of "containing mother"—despite attempts to work systemically. Staff inadvertently parented the families, who were seen as deprived and disadvantaged and desperately in need of help and advocacy. At the very beginning, transference-based group-relations interpretations were employed in the large group, which consisted of up to thirty-five children and adults of all ages. These techniques were dropped very quickly, triggered by an incident when, following what seemed an extremely "good" complex group interpretation, considerable chaos ensued. One child ran out of the unit and along the garden walls, parents and staff in hot pursuit, with the child ending up eventually on the roof of the main building! It seemed that a more concrete approach was needed, with the parents being actively in charge of their children rather than getting lost in the subtleties of the staff's interpretative work.

As families were perceived by staff to have overwhelming needs, they were expected to attend the Family Day Unit for approximately eighteen months. This also in part reflected the belief that change was a slow process. Somehow families obliged and paced themselves according to the staff's expectations. Their first month in the Family Day Unit, five days per week from 9 a.m. to 5 p.m., was usually turbulent: families and their individual members tended to display vividly the complex problems and issues that had brought them to the Marlborough. This was followed by them gradually settling down and becoming familiar, if not over-familiar, with the institutional ethos, the routines, and likely thera-peutic interventions—enough to provide staff with sufficient encouragement to remain interested. It slowly became apparent that families felt almost too comfortable attending week after week, month after month. Inevitably lethargy set in, with staff also feeling perhaps too comfortable and mutual paralysis setting in. A frequent observation was that around one month before the agreed discharge date, often during Month 16, families became restless, and new—or familiar—crises started happening again. It seemed that more active therapy could take place. However, on reflection it became obvious that an average stay of eighteen months was likely to encourage chronic relationships with staff, who found it increasingly difficult to remain in a meta-position and whose therapeutic effectiveness appeared to decrease every month. Fami-lies were reluctant to leave since they seemed to have found a new large "family" in the shape of the day unit, with sibling families and parental staff. After a few years of experimenting with this eighteen-month programme, it was decided to remove most of the "chronic" middle months, and the programme was shortened to three months.

Phase 2:   Hot-house phase

Structural family therapists maintain that change commonly occurs when the usual limits of the intensity of family interactions are exceeded (Minuchin, 1974). This can be done by increasing or shortening the time, pace, and focus of such interactions, and the programme of the Family Day Unit was deliberately designed to introduce such changes. In this way, the unit acted like a pressure cooker. Bringing things to the boil, so to speak, produces crises, often conveniently termed "therapeutic", based on the belief that they provide opportunities for change. The confrontation with an impasse in a therapeutic hot-house can lead individuals and fami-lies to experiment with new behaviours or solutions. However, inducing therapeutic crises can be a somewhat risky venture, with the potential of resulting in chaos or dangerous situations. Staff in the day unit were aware that after a challenging day these families had to go back to their own homes and that there was a considerable risk that they might "act out", or rather re-enact, destructive scenarios. In order to address this potential risk, a kind of safety-net was created in the form of an on-call rota. Families could access staff after hours and on weekends via a hospital switchboard and bleep system. If activated in this way, a member of staff would come out immediately and undertake some crisis-intervention work in the home. It has to be stated that another major reason for creating an out-of-hours response team was the team's wish to prevent other agencies, notably those believed to be non-systemic and therefore "linear", from intervening unhelpfully—for example, by sectioning a parent or removing a child via an Emergency Protection Order in the middle of the night. It was the team's view at the time that families had to be rescued from the traditional agencies of social control—notably social workers, police, and psychiatrists.

It was only when the team audited the number of calls at night and at weekends, mostly from single parents, that the whole concept of a crisis-intervention service was questioned. It seemed that some families had decided that they should have their crises out of hours, and that this enabled them to have special relationships with some staff. Moreover, it seemed that the mere existence of a crisis-intervention team had created a context of instant availability which lent itself to misuse. Some single parents had discovered that they could combat their loneliness by apparently being "in crisis" and thus accessing so-called help whenever required. Far from providing solutions to these families' "learnt helplessness", this stance was reinforced by inputs that could only result in confirming further their sense of inadequacy. Once this and other patterns of misusing the bleep-and-rota system had become evident, families were required to restrict their crises to ordinary office hours—unless they chose to run the risk of being dealt with by traditional professionals specializing in social-control types of interventions. Interestingly, most families obliged, and the absence of an emergency-response team contributed to more intensive work throughout the day.

The daily structure of the Family Day Unit programme very much reflected the wish to create maximum intensity, demanding of families to make many and repeated transitions in the course of

Table 3.1: Family Day Unit programme

Time	Monday	Tuesday	Wednesday	Thursday	Friday
8.45–9.30	Families arrive and settle	Families arrive and settle	Families arrive and settle	Families arrive and settle	Parents arrive and settle
9.30–10.00	Planning meeting	Planning meeting	Planning meeting	Planning meeting	Planning meeting
10.00–11.00	Parent-and-child activities	Multi-family activities	Parent-and-child activities	Outings to super-markets, parks, museum, etc.	Couple work
11.00–12.00	Individual family meetings	Adults' meeting Children's group	Individual family meetings		Adults' group
12.00–13.00	Lunch	Lunch	Lunch	Lunch	Lunch Staff reflections
13.00–14.30	Multi-family activities	Multi-family activities	Multi-family activities	Multi-family activities	Reflections meeting
14.30–15.00	Review meeting	Review meeting	Review meeting	Review meeting	
15.00–	Families leave	Families leave	Families leave	Families leave	Parents leave

24

the day and week. These transitions required everyone to change, within the space of a few hours, from being a member of one subgroup to that of another, such as being a member of his or her own family, peer group, work group, group of families, and so on. This provided an intense experience of changing contexts, with the opportunity to learn to cope with the resulting demands and difficulties. Individuals and families simply had constantly to change roles and behaviours in different settings. The theory behind this design was that, in the face of such demands, it would be difficult to hold on to familiar patterns of interaction, thus providing ample opportunities for experimenting with new behaviours. Staff also had to shift their roles and relationships, especially in relation to the adult members of the families: at one moment they were therapists, and a few minutes later they found themselves sharing some cooking tasks with the same client. Table 3.1 shows the week's programme.

The day begins with parents settling their children after the journey to the unit and informally talking to staff and other families. There then follows the *Planning Meeting*, chaired by one member of staff, with all families present in the same room. Each family states why they have come that day and what particular issues they wish to tackle. This can include how to play appropriately with one's child; how to stop granny from taking over all the time; how to be consistent; how to mange anger differently and so on. The discussion focuses on how these self-stated aims can be implemented during the course of the day—and how this might be done in the various contexts available. The *Parent-and-Child Activities* are structured age-appropriately for each family, who, on their own, undertake a joint task. Examples include: making a family out of clay; a dice game; face painting; cooking biscuits; and so on. The twice-weekly *Adults' Meeting* allows the parents to have some time for themselves, discussing issues that they regard as adult and therefore not for the consumption of children. At the same time, children may have a *Children's Meeting* which, depending on their ages may consist of viewing and talking about a video; doing some joint art work, or have some structured discussions. Lunch is prepared by the parents, occasionally jointly for all the families, but mostly individually for their own families. *Family Meetings* take place once-weekly at least, though over the years this work has become much less formal, with shorter sessions—lasting no longer than ten or fifteen minutes—being scheduled ad hoc during the day. Examples of *Multi-Family Activities* are described in chapter five. The *Review Meeting* and *Reflections Meeting* are both described in more detail later in this chapter.

During this phase, the work of the Family Day Unit was inspired and supervised by Salvador Minuchin, who spent a total of more than a year on two separate occasions at the Marlborough Family Service. The content and style of the therapeutic work at that time reflected his ideas. Once the emergency-response system had been abandoned, all therapy was carried out inside the Family Day Unit, which was seen as a hot-house promoting rapid growth. Very little home-based or outreach work took place during this phase. However, once a year all the families and staff went together on a five-day "holiday", in a rented house near the seaside, providing a highly intensive living experience, twenty-four hours a day. This allowed for much more intensive work to take place, and it seemed hardly like a holiday, certainly not for staff. After years of convening this annual event, it was eventually dropped and attempts were made to convert the upper floor of the building within which the Marlborough is located into two self-contained apartments so that twenty-four-hour work was occasionally possible when required. In the event, despite many promises from managers and politicians, the necessary funding and planning permission was never granted.

Phase 3: Network phase

The multi-family work carried out in the Marlborough Family Day Unit entered a new phase in the early 1980s. Inspired by the Milan team's paper "The Problem of the Referring Person" (Selvini Palazzoli et al., 1980), the team started focusing on the professional context within which the work was carried out. The view of the Family Day Unit as a safe haven, separate and very different from all the other services locally on offer, was abandoned, with the realization that the Marlborough was part of "the system" and that the professional network was part of "the problem". Regular visits by Luigi Boscolo and Gianfranco Cecchin to the Marlborough helped to review the focus of the work as well as learning to construct elaborate hypotheses on which the interventions could be based. A decision was made that any therapeutic work with complex families should be preceded by network meetings. Invitations to attend these were not only issued to all the various different professionals, but also to the family and to anyone the family regarded as *their* relevant network. These meetings were initially very much feared by the referring professionals, who were concerned that their thinking and work might be challenged or exposed via a series of "tricky" Milan-inspired questions. In those days, the Marlborough team still held on to the belief that they were "meta", and in so doing they sometimes gave the impression that this also meant "better". Both the structure and the content of these network meetings have been significantly modified over the years, with one of the aims being to counteract this unhelpful and arrogant notion. Meetings now last on average 90 minutes and are chaired by a Family Day Unit worker. The aim is to map the significant relationships within the family–professional network, to understand each person's concerns and to come up with an action plan, clearly spelling out aims, duration, and focus of the work of the day unit. A series of questions (Table 3.2) designed to elicit information provides the framework for the network meeting, and significant professionals who are unable to attend the meeting are asked to address these questions prior to the meeting so that their views can be represented.

At the end of the network meeting, it is the aim to have clear decisions as to which professionals should remain involved and which should not. The following points are defined as clearly and openly as possible:

• the specific tasks to be addressed;

• the frequency and purpose of meetings;

• the time-scale, including review meetings;

• the specific areas of change which should be targeted;

• a clear understanding of the consequences of change or no change as far as family and professionals are concerned.

Table 3.2: Network-Meeting Framework

Questions to Professionals

What is the reason for your involvement?

What are the main concerns you have in relation to the child, adult, family?

What do you see as their main strengths?

How often do you see whom, and what is the purpose of these meetings?

What would happen if these meetings did not take place?

How would you describe your relationship with the family?

How, in your opinion, does the family view your involvement?

What is your view of our service getting involved?

What should be the aims and time-scale of our involvement?

What do you think is the desirable and likely outcome of the work?

What would have to change for you to consider rehabilitation of the child(ren) to the family?

Questions to the Family

What is your understanding as to why we are having this meeting?

Which of the points put forward by the professionals do you agree with?

Which concerns do you not agree with?

Which helper is responsible for what aspect of your family and/or life?

How come that all these people are involved in your life?

Of all these people—who is the most/least helpful?

If one of the professionals disappeared suddenly from your lives—whom might you miss most/least?

How likely are you/your family to make the changes required?

What would you have to do to get all these professionals off your back?

What, in your view, might you be getting out of working with us?

What might be your own aims?

It may be necessary to draw up a three-way contract between referring agency, family, and Family Day Unit, formalizing the aims, content, and time-scale of the work. Following the network meeting, families are shown around the day unit and the work is explained informally and in quite concrete terms. If other families are present, newcomers can interview them about their experience. Many new families are quite apprehensive, because of issues of privacy and confidentiality, when they first hear that there are other families attending at the same time. In practice, when first arriving, parents tend to remain apprehensive and cautious as to what they should and should not reveal about themselves. Thankfully, children are usually much less inhibited and soon act as bridges between families. It is extremely rare for families to remain in isolated positions for more than a day or two. To their own surprise, after a very short time the vast majority of families find it a relief to be open in front of fellow strugglers about their difficulties.

The increased awareness of the importance of context led the team to design a systemic questionnaire (see Figure 3.1), which required clinicians to record in some detail specific family interactions. Based on these, it was possible to highlight repetitive interaction patterns that families themselves identified as problematic. Each family worker had to construct two structural family maps, representing the present picture as seen by the worker—the *present snapshot*—and another map to pinpoint change—the *change vision*—based on the information that family members provided as to how they wanted things to be different in the near future. Family workers were then asked to construct elaborate three- or four-generational systemic family hypotheses and then to consider in some detail how change could be promoted through the various activities in the programme. The purpose of this weekly exercise was to familiarize staff with systemic ideas and application of them to families attending daily in a specific setting. It required staff to think continually about how specific contexts—such as the various activities of the day unit programme, outings, or home-based work—could be utilized to help families explore new ways of dealing with familiar issues. It also helped staff not to become complacent about the programme in place, but to question its relevance for each of the families. This implied continually searching

Section 1
What are the observed behaviours, both "positive" and "negative", in the various day unit or home contexts? How could the interactions be described?

    Observed Behaviour   Contexts   Interactions

Section 2
Describe target behaviour/symptom/problem

Section 3
What are the effects of the target behaviour and the interactions around it?

Section 4
What does each family member/professional do to affect the target behaviour/symptom?

Section 5
Draw a structural map (*depicting family relationships, hierarchies, conflicts, boundaries, etc.*) or "snapshot" of

    a.   family and professionals as you see it at this point
    b.   how the family would like to be in three months

Section 6
Provide a three- or four-generational systemic hypothesis

Section 7
What minimum changes would need to be made for the target behaviour to change?

Section 8
What contexts would need to be utilized/created to address these issues?

planning meetings	family sessions
family activities	home-based work
multi-family activities	outreach work
nursery activities	network meetings
individual meetings	other working contexts

Section 9
What are the long-term issues for the therapeutic work with this family and social network?

FIGURE 3.1: Family Day Unit Systemic Questionnaire

for and identifying new contexts that might be made use of or had to be created, so as to address *in vivo* the particular issues that families and/or workers had identified.

A few examples may illustrate the potential usefulness of this questionnaire. Under Section 1, workers are required to enter observed interactions, such as:

Observed Behaviour	*Interactions*
Mother lights cigarette and stares into empty space	Johnny climbs up on chair. Jumps down
Mother seems lost in her thoughts	Johnny shouts, tries to "fall off" chair
Mother stares at wall	Johnny falls over and cries
Mother jumps up and shouts: "I told you not to do that"	Johnny cries and puts arms out to mother
Mother holds him	Johnny calms down and hugs mother

This example illustrates the specific features of one interactional sequence. The worker will then be required to note the specific contexts within which such behaviours occur. In the clinical discussion, attention will be drawn to other contexts when such sequences do not happen, and staff will be encouraged to generate hypotheses that are context-focused.

Section 2 of the systemic questionnaire invites the worker to enter the particular problem or target issue that the family itself has identified. The creation of this category was in part a response to the multiple presentations—as seen by the family and its individual members as well as by referring agencies and other professionals. In order not to be totally overwhelmed by the sheer number of possible problems or target issues, the team decided to work only with one such issue at the time. This involved meticulous negotiations with families as to what they themselves wanted to work on. Needless to say, this was easier said than done, given that many of the families claimed, when first meeting them, that there was absolutely nothing wrong with them and that they had had, in their view, a happy life until social services invaded it and caused trouble. In such circumstances families are asked to identify what, in their view, might be the one thing that, if it changed, would be likely to result in social services taking a bit more of a back-seat ("What do you think bothers the social workers most? What would happen if you did that differently—or is it important for you to have them in your lives? What would you have to do so that they would lose interest in your family?"). It is almost always possible to create an initial focus for work by giving families some responsibility in the way described.

Under Sections 3 and 4, staff are asked to speculate about the various effects that the "problem" has on the various interactions (intra-family as well as inter-families as well as between family and professionals) and how the respective responses generate or maintain the problem-determined system.

Section 5 is designed to address the workers' prejudices and perceptions. Structural maps are constructed by therapists, reflecting their perception of family structures and being organized by specific concepts in relation to hierarchies, boundaries, and relative distances between family members and professionals. Such a map can be likened to a Polaroid photograph, imprecise and fast, with all the good and bad characteristics of a snapshot. Like a snapshot, a structural map has some value in that it depicts a temporary frame which invites reflection and dialogue. The construction of a similar "change-vision" map, drawn up in conjunction with families, reflects the process of co-constructing a joint vision of change.

Under Section 6, staff are required to generate as many hypotheses as possible—to foster and practice systemic thinking. This section of the questionnaire was largely inspired by the input from the Milan team.

Under Sections 7 and 8, staff consider how, when, and where to intervene in the identified interaction sequences and patterns that appear to maintain the presenting problems. As therapeutic interventions always take place in a context, staff have to look at the many different activities of the day unit programme and identify the appropriate sites. This is a very pragmatic translation of systemic ideas into action.

Under Section 9 staff are invited to take a meta-position in relation to their own direct present involvement and therapeutic work and to consider the medium- and long-term issues likely to arise during family work. This may lead to reflecting about the advantages and disadvantages of involving members of the extended family or may address issues to do with the family's social and cultural network.

Phase 4: Outreach phase

The focus on the professional context brought with it an increased interest in the world outside the therapeutic setting, such as the community and the family's own home. While the team had from time to time seen families in their home, this was usually only in response to crises. Some families who did well during their time in the Family Day Unit would claim that it was impossible to transfer into their home environment changes made in the day unit. The issue of how families could export their experiences to their own home settings led to a significant increase of home-based work. Visiting the families' homes also allowed the team to take in the wider context of their lives—their neighbourhood, for example. Walking through dimly lit corridors in high-rise buildings, with lifts broken down, the stench of urine, disposed needles, racist graffiti all in evidence—all provides another aspect of what also seemed to be many of the families' daily reality. Staff could not but acknowledge the poor social circumstances and poverty in which these many families live. Somehow it seemed much less surprising that these families lived isolated lives, ashamed perhaps to invite others to witness the level of their deprivation. Hostile environments hardly encourage families to visit one another. In connecting with the daily struggles with families living such circumstances, it seemed quite difficult to retain a meta-position: how could one not be morally outraged about the social injustices that precipitated or contributed to these families' predicaments. The team decided that working systemically meant also working with the social context and becoming involved in more concrete issues, such as housing, financial matters, local anti-racist groups, and so on. No longer did it seem relevant to connect families with each other only in the relative luxury of our Family Day Unit, but a lot of work had to be carried out in the community—homes, community centres, neighbourhoods. Families were encouraged to make use of one another in order to rehearse new and unfamiliar situations, such as issuing invitations for visiting one another.

The common problem of poor housing found among the families attending the Family Day Unit led the team to tap into the hidden theatrical talents of many of the parents. They were asked to role-play hostile council workers and helpless and underprivileged parents. It was and is always a total surprise to discover how naturalistically many of the parents can impersonate hostile council workers and other officials. In such role-plays, families coach each other on how to respond differently and more effectively to the predictable responses of officials. Armed with these experiences, many families find that they are much better equipped to take on the "real world" successfully.

Carrying the experiences home, as a kind of "therapeutic takeaway", seemed increasingly important. The team learned to work in different home environments, and this gradually increased their confidence to tackle issues wherever they presented themselves. Subsequently, quite a bit of the work started taking place in public settings, such as supermarkets, pubs, community centres, the underground—and, of course, streets. Tackling, for example, the issue of uncontrollable toddlers who dangerously run into the middle of the road is not only easier if it can be studied "*in vivo*"—with the therapist on site—but also less persecutory when quite a number of families are present, some of whom are having to cope with similar behaviours of their own children. Filming such outings and then reviewing them afterwards in a multi-family setting elicits expert help from other parents.

Phase 5:   Expert phase

As the Marlborough Family Day Unit gathered more expertise and became better known, it tended to attract progressively more difficult and complex families. Increasingly families in which severe abuse had occurred were referred, first from the whole London area, later from all over south-east England. Social workers, guardians *ad litem*, and courts discovered that the unit was good at carrying out family and parenting assessments; for a variety of reasons, including economic ones to do with the survival and growth of the Marlborough Family Service, such referrals were accepted. Many of these families, threatened with permanent removal of their children, did not attend voluntarily, and it required considerable skill and expertise to engage them in therapeutic work. This led to more referrals, and over the past ten years families involved in Care Proceedings have become the main clientele of the Family Day Unit. These families know that they are being referred primarily to have their "parenting capacity" assessed. They also know that the day unit team has been asked to submit a detailed report on the quality of the parenting and family relationships, including their ability to change. This report makes recommendations to the court as to whether the children should or should not be separated from their parents.

Undertaking these assessments can be a tough task not only for the families but also for the workers. Seeing many seemingly "hopeless" families can be disheartening, particularly when all that seemed required was to rubber-stamp the local authority's decisions. Yet, despite the complexity of the families and their helping systems, much work in seemingly hopeless situations was quite successful. This was particularly so once the request for a parenting assessment was reframed as an invitation to see whether families could change. Despite strong beliefs at the outset that they would never be able to talk about their secrets of sexual or physical abuse in front of other families, many parents and children started exchanging experiences with one another and to have them validated by other parents and their children.

Nevertheless, as far as the day unit staff were concerned, the almost exclusive work with families with serious abuse histories did take its toll, with signs of "burn-out". It seemed no longer possible to run the day unit programme all year round—staff needed a break from time to time, and therefore experiments were tried with a whole range of different time frames—from three months to six weeks to one-week "modular" programmes. This was in response to an increase in staff sickness and demoralization.

The day unit currently has three full-time family workers, all with systemic training and recruited from a variety of different professions, such as nursing, social work, residential work, and psychology. There is also a total of two sessions of supervision and consultation provided by other members of the multidisciplinary team.

At present, families attend for about three months: an initial week, then only one day per week for the following two weeks, then another full week, then again just one day per week, followed by another intensive week. Home-based work is carried out in between these intensive day-unit-based weeks. The emphasis on assessment work, commissioned by social services or the courts, has of course affected our work, which usually takes place within a statutory and legal framework. The children attending with their parents are usually on Care Orders, and many will be placed with foster carers when first attending the day unit.

Referral to the Marlborough Family Day Unit is often seen as the parents' "last chance" to prove that they are "good enough" to have the children reunited with them, or that they are able to make sufficient changes so that rehabilitation becomes likely. Not surprisingly, most families are initially reluctant to attend. However, they tend to engage quickly, particularly once they have connected with other families who are likely to have had similar multi-agency involvement. There is a policy of total openness: all observations—no matter whether parents are likely to construe them as being positive or negative—will be shared, and families are at all times informed as to what staff think about the assessment to date and the possibility of rehabilitation of children with their parents. This encourages reflection and feedback, potentially promoting change. Similarly, the team encourages continuous feedback from families so that staff are able to examine their own assumptions, in the hope that this will also help to make the work more tailored to the needs of the families. Many parents have, over the years stated that this was the first place they had ever been to where staff are "totally straight . . . it's not always comfortable, but at least we know what you think". The Family Day Unit provides detailed reports for social services and the courts, and the observations and findings are constantly shared with the parents ("If we had to write the report on you today, we would say a, b, and c and you may think that this is not very positive . . . if you want us to write a different report, you have to make a few changes").

Apart from giving regular, open, and honest feedback to families at the end of each day, once a week a *Reflections Meeting*—inspired by Tom Andersen's (1987) reflecting-team ideas—is held. This takes place at the end of each week, on Fridays. While families are having their lunch, the three full-time family workers hold a clinical meeting, exchanging information and views about how each family has done during the past week. Staff discuss each family in turn, for approximately five minutes, reflecting on what has happened during the course of the week. The workers are very specific about their observations, listing a whole range of behaviours and interactions and speculating about underlying patterns. No attempt is made to be strategic, nor is there a sole focus on what families themselves might regard as positive feedback. Staff are aware that they might also make comments that could be perceived as critical by the families concerned. The style of this meeting is conversational, with workers triggering one another's ideas and reflections by comparing observations and ideas.

This staff discussion lasts about thirty minutes and is videotaped. The videotape recording of this session is then handed to a systemic consultant—Eia Asen or another senior clinician from the Marlborough—who has not been party to the staff's reflections, but who then straight away chairs the Reflections Meeting. In that sense the systemic consultant is in the same position as the families—knowing that a staff discussion has taken place but not knowing what has actually been said. The family workers are not in the room for the Reflections Meeting (although some will watch it via a video-link). This is deliberate as it makes staff temporarily unavailable for being drawn into prolonged discussions with families, feeling that they have to justify what they have said in their staff meeting. It thus allows staff to be in a reflective position, having to listen to the families' reflections without an opportunity to immediately putting the record straight. It also permits families to reflect on how staff might digest the parents' feedback to what has been said about them.

When first experimenting with appropriate structures for such reflections meetings some ten years ago, staff were present in the room—as an observing team. However, this position was difficult to maintain when parents challenged directly what staff had said—and staff then found it impossible not to immediately respond. This resulted in heated discussions as to which observation and comments were "correct" and which were not, with a non-reflective atmospheres prevailing on many occasions. Listening from behind a one-way screen to how families respond to the staff discussion is a very different experience, providing different perspectives for staff. It is not always an easy task, particularly when family workers believe that the systemic consultant is being manipulated by families into adopting "their" perspective, resulting in a split between consultant and family workers. The temptation to burst into the room and let the consultant know how "wrong" he or she got it can at times be considerable but is resisted at all cost. Any such differences would be confronted later in the post-reflections meeting.

The families and systemic consultant hold the Reflections Meeting in a room with a TV screen and video-recorder, as the videotape of the staff discussion will be played during the meeting. For a variety of reasons children are generally excluded from this meeting. This allows parents to focus on what is being said about their own families without being distracted by children, who tend to get bored just listening to a discussion that usually takes two hours. It also respects boundary issues in that some of the information would be inappropriate for younger children. Teenagers may be encouraged to attend the meeting—if they and their parents regard this as appropriate. Children usually have their own meeting, with one or two members of staff present; the meeting takes the form of playing games, watching a relevant film, or being part of a structured children's group with access to play materials.

At the beginning of the Reflections Meeting, the systemic consultant will ask parents whether they themselves want to discuss any specific issues that had come up during the week. They may also be asked to speculate about what, in their view, staff might have said in their discussion, which is about to be screened. Responses to this invitation vary: there are occasions when parents and older children are very eager to hear, as soon as possible, what has been said about them by the workers. On other occasions, their own agendas prevail and lively discussions ensue. The systemic consultant then starts the videotape and hands the remote control to one of the parents, usually one whose family is discussed by staff. Implied in this move is the message that it is up to the parent(s) to let the specific tape segment run for its entirety or to pause so that specific points can be taken up. Most parents opt for stopping and re-starting, often encouraged to do so by other families and the systemic consultant. Pausing the tape allows the families to respond immediately to the staff's reflections—dealing with continuous feedback is one of the aims of the meeting.

It is the systemic consultant's task to stimulate the families' curiosity about one another, as well as to encourage them to provide advice, criticism, and support. At the outset, the systemic consultant may be rather active, asking another parent to say what he or she thinks of what the staff have said ("What do you think about staff saying that Mary's cup of tea seems to be more important than feeding her child? Do you agree or not? What have you observed?"). Other parents are then brought in ("Can you respond to what Bill has said . . .").

Parents tend to support each other, particularly when staff are being perceived as being too critical. However, frequently it can also be observed that the staff discussion triggers the parents' own ideas of what the families could do differently in the future. Parents seem often more able to take advice from each other rather than from so-called "experts". A technique used by the systemic consultant prior to screening a specific video clip is to get different parents to speculate as to what, in their view, staff could or might have said about a family—their own or another. Their predictions will then be discussed in the light of what was actually said, leading to useful reflections. Inviting families to reflect about the reflections of staff regarding their own performance and that of other families is no doubt a complex activity. First, it puts the family under discussion temporarily in a meta-position in relation to their behaviours in our day unit. Moreover, it puts them in a position of help in relation to other families while at the same time giving them a voice that may inform staff as well.

The Reflections Meeting is a popular event, at times more so with families than with staff. Families like the idea that not only they themselves but also staff can be observed at work. This adds considerably to the ethos of openness and transparency prevailing in the Family Day Unit—seeing that staff are at times struggling to make sense, that they can be quite uncertain or puzzled, and that families' involvement and feedback is crucial for the work being successful.

The post-reflections meeting is of great importance for all staff, creating the loop of reflecting on the families' reflections of the staff's reflections. The systemic consultant and family workers discuss issues that have been brought up in the meeting and suggestions that families may have made leading to perhaps a new or different focus for future work. Family workers also reflect on the interactions between the families and the systemic consultant, including how she or he might have become inducted into forming an alliance with some parents against staff. As the Reflections Meeting is also videotaped, family workers can use clips to look at such interactions in detail, with the workers consulting to the consultant. Generally, this is usually regarded as a good mutual learning experience by all concerned.

Follow-up work

At the end of the contracted work, a review meeting is held involving the professionals and the family's network. Here, the team's views and recommendations are discussed. Families are never surprised to hear what the team has to say, due to the daily feedback during their attendance at the Family Day Unit. Further therapeutic work is done with families if appropriate, building on changes that have been made. However, in a number of cases the team recommends permanent separation of the child(ren) from the parents, and in such situations the focus of work will be on separating, planning contact visits, and possible individual or couple work with the parents once the children have been permanently separated from them.

Case illustration

Referral information

Jill, in her mid-30s, is a lone mother with three children. At the age of 10 years she was diagnosed by the local child psychiatric services as suffering from depression. She received some help at the time, but when 14 she took an overdose. She was admitted for a period of nine months to an adolescent unit where she disclosed sexual abuse by her stepfather. After discharge she was placed with foster-carers. Further episodes of clinical depression were diagnosed subsequently for which Jill received a considerable number of different antidepressants, followed by two inpatient admissions. At the age of 18, Jill went to college. There she seemed unable to make friends. She had a few brief relationships with abusive men and then met Paul, who became the father of her three children. He never lived with the family because he said that he needed to look after his dying mother. Shortly after the birth of her last child, Jill discovered that Paul had in the past spent some time in prison, having been convicted of sexual abuse of children. She immediately cut off all contact, and she and her children never saw him again. Jill subsequently discovered that her oldest child had been sexually abused by Paul.

The family were referred to the Marlborough Family Service by their social worker after the local authority had instituted Care Proceedings. There had been increasing concerns regarding Jill's ability to care appropriately for her three children. Bill, the eldest, was 8 years of age, presenting as a disruptive child at school, with threats of permanent exclusion. He was described as being either very "high" or very "depressed". He had also started setting fires both at home and at school. The younger of the two boys, Tom, who was 6 years old, had been diagnosed as suffering from epilepsy and learning disability, requiring him to attend a special school. He needed constant supervision as his behaviour could be quite unpredictable, including dangerous behaviours in the roads. Molly, the 3-year-old girl, who was bright and very lively, presented in her nursery with behavioural problems. She was reported to bite other children, particularly when she was feeling ignored.

Network meeting

The initial network meeting revealed the involvement of a considerable number of workers, some of whom were quite unaware of their colleagues' inputs. Altogether twenty-one different profes-

sionals, representing the health, the education, and the social services, were attached to this family, with relatively little—if any—
communication and coordination between the various agencies
and many different opinions on how this mother and her children
could best be helped. Jill was not only confused but also paralysed
by all the expert opinions and somehow unable to know what her
own expertise, if any, was.

The first family meeting took place in the family home, a damp
two-bedroom flat in bad state of repair, on the seventh floor of a
run-down housing estate. The visit provided an opportunity to
study family interaction *in vivo*, with mother struggling in the
kitchen preparing a meal while the children became involved in a
major fight, each claiming that the other had started it. Jill found
this all too much and ended up locking herself in the toilet. This
was followed by Bill lighting a small fire in the bedroom. His
brother shouted "Fire, fire", and Jill immediately rushed out of the
bathroom and extinguished the flames expertly. Jill turned to the
team and said: "I'm glad you're here . . . now someone can really
understand what I have to deal with every day."

Family Day Unit attendance

A week later, the family attended the Family Day Unit. Jill was
initially very reluctant to make contact with the five other families
present at the same time. She sat in a corner as her own children
played with other children. It was noticeable how the more her
children engaged in play with the children of other families, the
more withdrawn and "switched off" Jill became. All her three
children became increasingly louder and "hyperactive", as if to
stimulate their mother into "waking up" and taking action. It was
only once Bill got into a fight with two other children that Jill was
asked by one of the fathers, "Do something!" Jill felt very embar-
rassed and criticized. She said so but, at the same time, she took
charge of her children. A day later, another mother challenged Jill:
"Your kids have to be wild to switch you on." Jill's first reaction
was shock, but, with the help of other parents, she started to look
at how her own state of mind was affecting her children's responses. Two mothers in particular made some constructive suggestions in a way that Jill could take their advice, and she began to

experiment with new ways of dealing with her children's provocative behaviours. Jill now regularly talked to other parents and children, including exchanging telephone numbers with three of the other parents attending the Family Day Unit.

Outreach work

An outing to the supermarket—which was filmed with the family's knowledge and permission on a small camcorder—provided more information about Jill's difficulties in keeping each child in mind while crossing streets, choosing food, and struggling with her children's unruly behaviour in public places. As this shopping trip involved three other families, there was ample opportunity of "live" observation and reflection on how things were going—with not only staff but above all other parents commenting on what they saw. Jill asked for advice, and some other parents made various suggestions. This required Jill to remain "switched on" (as she called it), and she attempted to use these ideas. Later on, back in the day unit, a video feedback session helped her and her children to look at the sequence of events from a different perspective and to identify different ways of dealing with the same scenario in the future. Other parents provided valuable reflections and suggestions.

Reflections Meeting

At the end of the week, in the Reflections Meeting, Jill listened intently to the staff's observations and views. When the systemic consultant invited her and the other families to respond, a lively discussion ensued. One mother in particular was very critical of how, in her view, Jill was allowing herself to be manipulated by her disabled child. Another parent, herself the mother of a disabled child, rallied to Jill's defence and made a special point about how one had to make special allowances for disabled children. This was immediately challenged by the father from a different family, who referred to the videotaped outing to the supermarket and how he had observed how the little boy had deliberately targeted his mother. The staff's reflections had acted as a catalyst, facilitating the conversation between different families regarding issues of disability and manipulation.

Home-based work

During the following three weeks, Jill and her children attended only once-weekly, for a whole day with four other families. Each week, there was also some home-based work, lasting either a whole morning or a whole afternoon. Jill reported that she had made friends with one of the mothers and that they had met a few times over the preceding weekend. She said that she found it helpful to hear what other people in "my situation do" and that she found their advice "much more helpful than all these professionals put together". During these days, both individual and family work took place, addressing how she could balance her own needs with those of the children, how much she identified with her disabled son, and how this revived memories in her of being "damaged" and abused in her own family of origin.

More Family Day Unit work

One month later, the family returned for another week to the Family Day Unit. Three new families had joined the programme, and Jill took it upon herself to make them feel welcome and explain what she had found useful during her last spell in the unit. She seemed much more "switched on", and this was reflected in the behaviour of her children, who had become less attention-seeking and generally more contained.

Some of the work now focused on how Jill could contribute to changing her housing situation. This was addressed in a multi-family activity through role-play, with other parents acting as tough officers from the local housing department or as unsympathetic social workers. Jill required some coaching from other parents on how to assert herself and how she could present herself differently so that she would be heard and be taken more seriously. She was also provided with specific "lines" on how to handle likely objections and on what tone of voice to adopt.

Follow-up work

Follow-up work with the family continued for another six months, with some home-based work, family sessions in our clinic, and further individual work with Jill (10 individual sessions in all). A two-year follow-up showed that in the eyes of the local social services department her parenting was now "good enough". All the children's names had been removed from the Child Protection Register but the social services department had remained involved, providing some practical support as well as rehousing the family. Jill had long stopped her antidepressants, and she reported that her—their—lives had the normal ups and downs but that the family was doing well.

The Marlborough Family Day Unit has a good record of engaging multi-problem families. The take-up rate is very high and the drop-out rate is low, possibly also reflecting the considerable pressure that families are under from social services and the courts to attend the day unit. In most of these families, serious child abuse and neglect are the major reason for referral and the staff are required to make recommendations as to the future placement of children. In about two-thirds of the cases, rehabilitation of the child(ren) with the family is recommended, with recommendations in the remaining one-third for permanent separation of the child(ren) from the family of origin. This latter figure may seem unusually high, but it reflects the Marlborough's reputation for dealing with the very severe end of the spectrum of child abuse.

Further developments

In an effort to vary the clinical work and not to become too typecast at only dealing with these type of issues, families presenting with different issues and problems have also been seen in the Family Day Unit. These have included families where a parent presented with serious mental health problem; families with disabled children; and families with children who have a serious chronic physical illness, specifically diabetes. Being able to work with these families over days has particularly helped the parents of these children to make contact with fellow sufferers. With families with diabetic children, for example, it has been possible to undertake work around meals and medication, addressing acute living problems in concrete ways.

The Marlborough Family Day Unit is probably the first of its kind. Over the years, many visitors from Europe, the Americas, Asia, and Australia have taken an interest in the work. It has been rewarding to observe how similar units have been created in different countries and how their work has evolved.

Prof. T. Fürniss and his team in Münster (Germany) focus their work on a well-defined sample of families with middle-class pre-school children who present with emotional or behavioural problems. This group of families very much reflects the affluent area within which this unit is located. Their purpose-built unit has been in operation since 1997 and has been highly successful, with full occupancy and a considerable waiting-list. Follow-up shows good symptomatic improvement as well as more general benefits for family functioning.

The family day unit in Dresden (Germany), led by Prof. M. Scholz and his team, was opened in 1998 and takes children aged between 4 and 14 years, usually presenting with serious behavioural and emotional disorders. Having studied the work of the Marlborough Family Day Unit, Prof. Scholz decided not to admit families where child abuse or neglect was the presenting problem or where there was heavy involvement from the courts. The unit operates five days a week from 8 a.m. to 3 p.m. all year round. Families stay, on average, six weeks. This project has become very popular and the results have been very encouraging, so much so that the pre-adolescent children's inpatient ward has been closed. The team discovered that there was no need to admit children for lengthy inpatient stays if the family became involved on a daily basis in the management and treatment of their problem child. The unit is now oversubscribed and has to operate a waiting list. The first effects on the German health system are already in evidence in that traditional child-psychiatry inpatient units are being asked to consider opening similar family day units.

Family day units were set up in the 1980s in Rotterdam (the Netherlands). In Scandinavia, colleagues from different parts of the region have over the past decades adapted the ideas from the Marlborough to both day and residential settings. Some residential units admit families for many months, with each family inhabiting their own flat within the institution. Some of the work is carried out with individual families and combined with cross-over work involving other resident families.

In Milan (Italy), a group of clinicians around Dr S. Cirillo, Teresa Bertotti, and Roberta Carini are about to open a multi-family project aimed at the type of families the Marlborough has become so well known for treating. This team has for many years treated and assessed abused children and their families who have been referred by the courts and social services (Cirillo & DiBlasio, 1992). The team is now evaluating outcome by comparing their well-researched standard approach with an experimental multi-family treatment package based on the Marlborough Family Day Unit.

All these units have quite different aims and structures, depending on the type of families they are working with and the social context. It is encouraging to see that many of the ideas of multi-family work are applicable in other countries and can be trans-created into different working contexts.

In Britain there are a number of institutions, funded by the health service or social services, offering residential facilities and in which some multiple family work goes on. However, in general, multiple family therapy is not regarded in this country as a major important ingredient of work with families.

In London, the Marlborough Family Day Unit has continued to change, by experimenting with many different ideas, time frames, and techniques. An "institution for change" (Cooklin et al., 1983) can simply not afford to do more-of-the-same—however tempting. The many new families that attend our day unit every year bring in novelty. Their curiosity and feedback challenge and stimulate the team, resulting in continuously evolving new structures.

CHAPTER FOUR

The Family School

Twenty years ago, Brenda McHugh and Neil Dawson were employed in the Family School to teach the children of the families who attended the Family Day Unit. However, after these therapists had been immersed in systemic practice for a period of time and trained in family therapy both at the Marlborough and at the Institute of Family Therapy, London, it became clear that there was a chance to develop the therapeutic potential of the Family School in its own right. There was a unique opportunity to use children's learning as a face-saving route to provide therapeutic help for families who might otherwise have shied away from the implied stigma or fears associated with therapy in its more usual format.

Originally, children attended the Family School on their own and rejoined their parents in the day unit after the teaching programme was finished. The first significant systemic initiative was an experiment in which a parent spent a session with his or her child in the Family School. This proved to be successful in promoting change, and so a process developed over the years of increasing the number of parents who would attend with their child at any one time. Today, the Family School is always full, with nine families taking part in the multi-family classroom every day (Dawson & McHugh, 1986a, 1986b, 1987, 1988, 1994).

The current Family School multi-family group model

The Family School programme is a multi-family group intervention. It provides therapy based in an education context as well as education anchored in a therapeutic relationship. As such, it creates a bridge between education and mental health (Plas, 1986). The children and families attend the Family School classroom together for four mornings each week. Children are referred by schools because of serious concerns about their psychological and behavioural difficulties. The unique feature of the Family School is that all children who attend have to be accompanied by at least one parent or other adult family member for the whole time. With a maximum of nine children at a time, this can mean that there are often more than twenty people present on any one morning.

Context

The Family School is housed in a single-storey building in the garden of the Marlborough. It is designed to function as a classroom, with the normal children's desks and educational equipment. In addition, within the classroom there is a kitchen area and a space with comfortable seating for the parents or other adults. There is a small office, which doubles as an interview-room, directly attached to the classroom. The classroom can be viewed from the office by means of a one-way screen.

The three Family School staff are all fully qualified teachers with experience of teaching in mainstream schools. In addition, two are senior family therapists and the other is an experienced educational therapist.

A classroom-based intervention

Designing a model of therapeutic practice set in a specialist class-room has been very effective in creating situations and opportuni-ties for systemic interventions with children and their families. Although it is most unusual for a large number of parents and children to be together in a classroom, being part of such a group has many positive effects.

Most parents talk about the embarrassment, shame, or guilt associated with having children who are always unhappy or getting into trouble. Often, such parents also describe desperate feelings of sadness and powerlessness in relation to their children if they are persistently experiencing serious difficulties at school; these difficulties may relate to their academic performance or to their relationships with teachers or with other children, or more usually a combination of all these. All referrals to the Family School are made on the basis that there are known or suspected significant intra-family problems in addition to the difficulties be-ing shown by a child at school.

One statement repeated many times by parents refers to feel-ings of having to manage problems with their children on their own, frequently in the face of criticism and opprobrium either from their own relatives or from professionals with whom they have become involved. Being part of a group of parents who are all struggling with similar difficulties is often highlighted as one of the major benefits of being at the Family School. Parents support each other but will also encourage one another to try new ways of doing things with their children. Although everything operates within a defined parent/teacher/pupil context, it is clear that the actual potential for beneficial influence extends well beyond this range to other familial contexts. Marital relationships, adults' self-views, intergenerational issues, and many other areas of family life are directly affected by participation in the multi-family intervention.

Basing the therapeutic programme in a classroom was in-tended to be a way of making a systemic model of practice acces-sible to more people. It was designed in such a context to enable teachers, educational psychologists, and education welfare officers connected with local schools to refer children more easily to this part of the Marlborough (Dowling & Taylor, 1989). Teachers in schools had previously said how difficult it often was to persuade families to allow themselves to be referred to a psychiatric provision, even a community-based one such as the Marlborough. Parents would tell the education professionals that they would not consider referral for a variety of reasons; they would commonly say that they did not see the link between their child having behavioural difficulties and the need for the family to go for treatment. Alternatively, parents would sometimes blame the school for their child's difficulties and would not accept the implication that they needed any help. Whatever the reasons, teachers were often very frustrated because of their inability to get the help they felt was appropriate for the children they were struggling with in school.

Disorientation

The first effect of having so many adults in the Family School classroom is that it makes the classroom—which looks like a classroom—not look like a classroom. Both the children and the adults are initially disorientated by the experience of being put together in this new and unfamiliar context. For the children, one effect is to make them more uncertain about employing their usual classroom behaviours. They are unable to pigeon-hole the teacher-therapists very easily and have to adjust their behaviour to accommodate to the novel interactional situation. Similarly, for the adults, the juxtaposition of the apparently familiar classroom organization with the uniquely unfamiliar expectations of their roles within that context creates opportunities for change. All parents who have attended the Family School report that they felt unsure of their position at first, and that they were not clear about what they were expected to do. The task of the teacher-therapists is to exploit the creative possibilities during this phase while at the same time providing sufficient certainty and clarity in order that the children and families do not become too disorientated and lose heart.

Mutual support

A further effect of having the multi-family group is the enormously powerful impact of parents talking together about their shared experiences. In many areas of disability involving children, parental support groups have proven to be very beneficial. Unfortunately, when children develop emotional or behavioural difficulties, the usual consequence is for them and their parents to become more isolated within the local community. This process tends to work against the possibility of setting up support groups for such families. The Family School creates the opportunity for parents to form mutual-support groups. Many families have stayed in contact with each other long after they have left the Family School.

Engaging prospective families using the multi-family group

The Family School staff originally made home visits when children were referred to the Family School. In the early years, this seemed to be the best way of approaching families to attempt to allay fears and persuade them to accept the referral. Recently the team has stopped doing such visits and has come to rely solely on the multi-family group to engage new families. Parents who are already attending the Family School are invariably the most effective in helping visiting parents and children to make the decision to take up a place. If the parents and children who are visiting and are understandably unsure about the potential benefits of attending are reassured by people who have experienced the place for themselves, they are more likely to take a chance that the Family School might be useful to them.

A new family is initially invited to visit the Family School so that they can find out what goes on there. It is explicitly stated that there is no expectation of a commitment to take up a place at this stage. The prospective family always comes during the morning programme when other children and their parents are present. They will see a busy classroom, with children and parents working together with the teacher-therapists. After a brief discussion with the visiting child and his or her parents, they are introduced to one or more of the parents who are already attending. The teacher-therapist leaves them alone together after the new family has been advised to find out about what actually happens and whether attending the Family School has been helpful. There is no doubt that, in the vast majority of cases, this is the single most effective element of the process of engaging new families in the Family School programme.

Isolation and feelings of hopelessness are repeated features of families referred to the Family School (Cooklin et al., 1983). This first meeting with a family who has been in the same position before attending the Marlborough but has experienced some change for the better is an excellent way of giving a new family some hope that things *can* get better. The pairing of families with similar presenting problems is one way of connecting "new" and "old" families. Pairings can be based on many other features, such as similar family-relationship difficulties—for example, divorce, violence, post-traumatic stress, bereavement, single-parent problems, three-generational discord, and so on. Even if there is no obvious relationship or life-cycle issue for the new and old families to share, there is always the common theme of a child who is having great difficulties at school. The pairing can then simply be based on a more hopeful old family and a defeated and pessimistic new family.

The multi-family group programme

The whole Family School programme is structured around a core multi-family group. Each school morning lasts for two and a half hours. There are two main strands to the programme: education and therapy. The aim has been to design a new way of working that provides a crossover between these two fields:

1. to blend the staff's teaching skills and knowledge with their family systems training and expertise;
2. to create a Family School that is recognizably educational but is also demonstrably therapeutic for families.

Each area of professionalism feeds the other in order to produce a dynamic whole with a focus on change.

Table 4.1 shows a typical weekly timetable.

Table 4.1: Family School Daily Timetable

Monday

09:30–10:10	First phase—teaching in relation to educational and behavioural targets.
10:10–10:40	Structured multi-family group; four minutes per family; weekend feedback.
10:40–11:00	Children and family break; parents solely in charge of children. Mid-morning planning meeting for teacher-therapists.
11:0–12:00	Second phase—teaching and cross-family linkage.

Tuesday

09:30–10:10	Teaching involving parent-and-child shared activity.
10:10–10:40	Multi-family group; theme-driven meeting.
10:40–11.00	Family break. Mid-morning planning meeting for teacher-therapists; issues discussed for parents' meeting
11:00–12:00	Parents' group. Children's group.

Wednesday

09:30–10:10	Teaching with parents observing.
10:10–10:40	Multi-family group; feedback on school behavioural targets.
10:40–11:00	Family break. Mid-morning planning meeting for teacher-therapists; multi-family-activity arrangements confirmed.
11:00–12:00	Multi-family activity.

Thursday

09:30–10:10	Teaching in relation to educational and behavioural targets.
10:10–10:40	Multi-family group; children's voices; plans for school and weekend.
10:40–11:00	Family break. Mid-morning planning meeting for teacher-therapists; pairings for cross-family linkage determined.
11:00–12:00	Teaching and cross-family linkage

First phase

At the initial network meeting, specific behavioural targets are negotiated between the teachers, the child, and their family. This helps to engage both the family and the school in monitoring progress and looking for change. Discussion of the children's psychological and behavioural symptoms in relation to school is the core reason for the multi-family group to meet together. Accordingly, the first part of a Monday morning session (9:30–10:10) consists of *teaching in relation to educational and behavioural targets* (Table 4.1). It is a time when the children are taught in the classroom with all their parents or other family members present. Depending on the presenting difficulty, parents can either sit with their children and help them or talk with the other parents in an informal group, still within the body of the classroom. Each child's targets provide the framework for observation and feedback. Despite the children's behaviour being the nominal focus of change, discussions throughout the programme also lead to targets being made explicit for the adults as well. The reciprocal nature of the parent–child interaction is always the central concern.

The task of teacher-therapists during this phase of the morning is to be both teacher and systemic therapist. This is achieved by teaching the children and observing and experiencing the difficulties that they present in this context. In the classroom, children will show their difficulties either in relation to their schoolwork or in their interactions with the teacher or with peers. In the particular setting of the Family School, there is the added dimension of being able to observe difficulties in the intra-family relationships.

When difficulties appear, teacher-therapists can change position from teacher to systemic therapist. The task is then to convert the teacher-observation into an interactional issue that is relevant to the child and his or her parent and to use it as a potential vehicle for change. This is very different from the usual position of teachers, who, when confronted with problematic behaviour, would expect to have to resolve the situation themselves. In the Family School, this would be seen as an opportunity missed, as there would be less potential for new information to be introduced to the child and family system as organized around an educational task.

The structured multi-family group meeting

After the initial "teaching" phase of the morning, all children and family members come together for a *structured multi-family group meeting* (Table, 4.1, 10:10–10:40). All the children, parents, other family members, and staff take part in the meeting. It lasts for thirty minutes and takes place at the same time every day. Each meeting is chaired by one of the teacher-therapists; the second works as co-therapist and the third acts as timekeeper. In turn, all the families are allocated their own four minutes for discussion, and this is divided into two parts. The family members can use the first two minutes as they wish, but they usually report back to the group on how the last twenty-four hours has gone in relation to their goals for change. For the next two minutes, the rest of the members of the group are invited to make comments related to this family. These can be about what has just been said, but they may also be about changes that somebody might have noticed or observations about how the child or parent has been trying something different or how the family members seem to be getting stuck with each other. The timekeeper lets everybody know when it is time to move on to the next family. During the first two minutes, it is the chair's responsibility to hold the structure of the meeting and occasionally to prompt the family reporting back to the group. For the second two minutes, the chair and co-therapy partner work together to manage the flow of information around the group. They can help to elicit and highlight themes as they come up, as well as encouraging the group members to become more expert in observing their own and others' repeating patterns of behaviour. The therapists attempt to create the conditions in which the different families can both challenge and support each other in their struggles for change.

Clearly, all that needs to be spoken about cannot be said in only four minutes per family. However, there are several interesting consequences of maintaining this tight time boundary. First, it helps to reduce the amount of redundant information in the meeting and encourages family members to focus more clearly on how they are going to use "their" time. It also requires the teacher-therapists to be disciplined in the nature and style of their interventions. The priority is to be economical and to facilitate inter-family communication. If the teacher-therapists intervene too much, they can become over-central, with a consequent reduction in potentially useful inter-family interactions. The Family School's practice is based on a structural model, and the multi-family group is an excellent context for intensification (Minuchin, 1974). Leaving a "hot" family issue at the end of the four minutes without a resolution invariably provokes charged discussion between the families after the formal meeting has ended. This is an example of a situation in which hidden therapeutic potential is derived from apparently unpromising circumstances, where time and availability is restricted by necessary organizational factors.

In a multiple family therapy group, there is often an extra feeling of immediacy and intensity that is not always easily attained in a more conventional family session. Moreover, the information raised in a multi-family group as it relates to one family frequently has significant meaning for other families in the group. Families often say that they have thought about something seen or heard in the group several days ago and have decided to try something different as a result. Over time, the multi-family group gains its own momentum and becomes a context that drives the participants to expect change in themselves as well as in other group members.

Applause is often given in the group for children or adults who are either reporting positive change or have been noticed to have done something differently during the meeting. At certain stages, children are encouraged to think about how they would like their parents to behave differently and to specify targets for them. One 6-year-old boy said that he would like his mother to stop talking to herself, to be calmer, and not to spend all her time cleaning the flat. Over time, he was able to report to the group that she had done very well and made good progress with her targets. As she got calmer, he became less worried about her and was soon able to go back to school full-time. Without a continual concentration on the mutuality of their relationship, it would not have been possible for the little boy to change on his own. When it dawns on the adults that they need to change if there is to be any hope that their children will change, the whole process gathers a pace and momentum of its own. It was only when the boy's mother fully appreciated the intertwined nature of her predicament and preoccupations with her son's anxieties and behaviour that she was able to make the necessary moves to support them both in a process of change.

When people are not changing, the rest of the group want to know why not and ask about what needs to happen for something to shift. This dynamism can lead to spirited exchanges that are not readily available in the professional–client relationship in therapy. It is far harder to ignore information from somebody who has painful first-hand knowledge of your predicament than from someone who is only "paid" to know about such things.

Mid-morning planning meeting

Half way through the morning the children have a break with their parents, and the staff have a *mid-morning planning meeting* (10:40–11:00), to discuss the day's programme. This planning is based on the issues or themes that have been raised in that day's multi-family group as well as in relation to observations of interactions during the first teaching phase of the morning. Potential pairings for cross-family linkage (see below) are discussed, and plans made for how they will be established and monitored by the teacher-therapists. The last hour of the morning (11:00–12:00) is another teaching/therapy phase and is a time to implement new ideas that have evolved during the earlier part of the morning. Parents may decide to sit with their child if there is an issue in the family to do with proximity, or those who are too closely involved with their children's activities may experiment with different degrees of separation. Children may try out different ways of asking for help, and their parents may be helped to practise not responding to old behaviours. Parents may help each other notice when they get caught out in redundant behaviour patterns. All activities are designed to maximize the potential for change in the family relationships.

Second phase—implementation

Again, as in the first period of the morning, the teacher-therapists alternate between the two professional roles available to them.

However, in this phase, the emphasis is more likely to be weighted more towards the therapeutic orientation than on the teaching component. On Wednesdays, *multi-family activities* are designed to look at issues within and between families that have emerged during the week's work. These are described in some detail in chapter six.

Cross-family linkage

After the break, on Mondays and Thursdays, *teaching and cross-family linkage* takes place, to implement points arising from the staff discussion.

In the Family School, parents are often encouraged to become actively involved with other children as well as with their own. This is an effective way of disrupting the predictability of the relationship for both the adult and the child. For the adult interacting with someone else's child, there is the likelihood that patterns familiar to their own child will be unfamiliar to the new one. Similarly, for the child, experiencing different interactions with another adult, who is neither their parent nor their teacher, can be a good opportunity for experimentation with new relational styles. Cross-family linkage therefore creates a unique opportunity in which adults and children cannot predict the responses of the other and so have the chance to be creative, with new communications and behaviours. Furthermore, the parent who is observing his or her child with another adult, has a chance to see how things could be different. Also, the child who is observing his or her own parent relating to another child is given a view of how there could be different possibilities for his or her own relationship.

For the teacher-therapists, cross-family linkage offers great potential for having a much wider variety of relationships available to work with. It is very helpful as a way of introducing novelty and difference into an overly fixed parent–child relationship. It is also another useful means to counteract the potential centrality of the teacher-therapist role.

On Tuesdays, after the break, there are separate *parents' groups and children's groups*. The parents' group allows the adults to discuss issues that they would not necessarily wish to raise in front of the children. These could range from how to deal with violent partners, to addressing issues of intimacy or how to manage parental guilt, through to discussions about practical problems associated with money or housing difficulties. Parents often question one another, but they also speculate about what the children might think if they were present at this meeting. This frequently leads to discussions about what is appropriate information to share with the child and what is not. In parallel to this parents' group is the children's group, which enables children to develop their own voices away from their parents. Play, metaphor, and games are used to elicit children's preoccupations. This group also lends itself to addressing peer-group issues.

A long-term slow open group

The multiple family group can be thought of as a long-term open group whose membership changes slowly over time. Children and their families are joining and leaving all the time. The composition of the group is continually changing, and this demands particular techniques to be employed by the staff. When there are new members joining, the teacher-therapists become more central and more actively manage the flow of information around the group. Once the group has become more established, the leaders can become less controlling and can focus more on promoting inter-family communications. This is done with a view to developing exploration of common themes shared by a number of families or to highlighting differences. The group offers an opportunity for change to be reported, noticed, and rewarded by acclamation. Through participation in this group, children and families are encouraged to become better observers of their own and others' behaviour patterns. This is often particularly noticeable when new families join and the experienced families pick up and comment on patterns and processes that are maintaining the problem. For the "old" families, it can be very reassuring and confidence-building to see new families arriving who are so obviously at an earlier stage than they are. It helps to make clear the distance they have come and the changes they have established during their time at the Family

School. Two things happen. First, the "old" family usually reassures the new one that they recognize the predicament that they are in and offer encouragement to stick the course. Second, these observations frequently help to persuade "old" families that it is time for them to leave.

The group goes through cycles of optimism and pessimism, through periods of rapid change and periods of apparent stagnation. The episodes of apparent stagnation usually occur just before a significant burst of positive activity in the group. This requires the professionals not to lose their perspective and become bogged down by a lack of optimism at any one time. Groups work well when at least two children and their families are starting to experience positive change. Their good feelings can be expanded to offer the hope that change is possible for the others as well.

Age range

The Family School accepts referrals of children of the normal school age range, from 5 to 16 years old. In practice, this means that the population of nine children attending the school on any one day can often cover a wide age range: 5-year-olds may be in the same classroom as 15- or 16-year-olds. This arrangement has several possible advantages. In the first place, it supports the observation that the Family School is not easy for the children to define. This is particularly helpful with older adolescents, who are likely to be familiar with the usual type of educational support provision often based on much narrower age bands.

The age range can also be helpful in relation to the parents of the children referred. The parents of the adolescents are often older than the parents of the younger children. They may feel more removed from the stage when their children were younger and are often able to give advice and insights from this different perspective. The parents of the younger children are often closer in age to the adolescents and are quite commonly more in touch with school, family, and community issues relevant to this age group. Having the full school-age range has also made it possible to have a number of siblings attending at the same time. This can have obvious benefits from a systemic point of view, but it can also be helpful in enabling hard-pressed parents to attend if the practical difficulties of having a number of children at different schools is seemingly too problematic.

Case illustration

Seven-year-old Mohammed had been referred to the Family School because his behaviour was unmanageable at his own school. He would hurt other children when they would not do what he wanted them to do. When challenged, he worried his teachers because even though he would admit what he had done he showed no signs of being sorry and would repeat the same sort of assault within minutes of the previous incident. His Moroccan parents, Aziz and Sameira, said that their son did things without thinking sometimes. However, the main problem was that even though he would behave well for his father, he wouldn't listen to his mother. In the Family School, Mohammed performed in very much the same way as described by his teachers. When being taught he would not listen to instructions and would argue with the teacher-therapists when they were functioning in the teacher mode. As the behaviour was happening, the teacher-therapist would stop teaching and use the event to develop a therapeutic discussion with Aziz or with Sameira. It was more usual for Sameira to come on her own with Mohammed, although Aziz would attend every so often; they rarely came together. At the beginning, Sameira would make excuses for Mohammed's behaviour and would develop elaborate, but unconvincing, explanations for his actions. He was variously tired, hungry, thirsty, unwell—or was really a good boy who was just misunderstood. Sameira was unable to set any clear limits or to restrict his behaviour and, when his actions became too provocative, would resort to empty threats and bamboozlement as attempts to gain some degree of control. On mornings when Aziz was with Mohammed, similar things would happen. Aziz would struggle with his son but use every way to appease him while at the same time denying that he was having any difficulty.

The conversations that resulted from these observations led to a disclosure in the multi-family group that Aziz and Sameira were living separately in the same house and that there was chronic tension and bitterness in their relationship. They were barely speaking to each other, and Mohammed and his younger brother were having to act as go-betweens. It was clear that the only way the boys could get their parents to speak to each other was by behaving badly. Sameira felt unable to separate fully from Aziz because she felt her two sons needed their father and that she would also be very isolated as a single parent in London. At the same time, she was also preoccupied with vengeful thoughts focused on her belief that Aziz should not be allowed to get away with his infidelity. Her extended family was still living in Morocco, and she felt very much the shame of having an unsuccessful marriage. Aziz also felt that it was important for him to remain at home so that he could help to bring up his sons.

Prior to this becoming known in the multi-family group, the other families were extremely angry and frustrated with Aziz and Sameira because they could not understand why neither parent would attempt to control Mohammed's behaviour or set any normal limits without making endless excuses for him. Once the knowledge was shared within the group of parents, the mothers in particular became much more sympathetic towards Sameira and became determined to help her see the harm that the bitter and unresolved marriage breakdown was causing everybody, and particularly the children. They supported her in moves to make a clear separation and regain some semblance of control in her life. Within the group of adults, there was a wide range of experiences of marital problems as well as personal understanding of different cultural attitudes to family and marital breakdown. Another Arab family in the group was particularly clear that keeping secrets from Mohammed and his brother was contributing significantly to their confusion and distress. The other families were not willing to accept Sameira and Aziz's proposition that the marital tensions were not adversely affecting the children. Many had painful first-hand experience of the damage caused to their children by acrimonious marital disputes.

Rather than the teacher-therapists needing to raise the relevant issues for Sameira and Aziz directly, it was much more powerful when they were discussed between the adults in the multi-family group. The professional's position became that of facilitator, whereby knowledge of each person's circumstances could be used to stimulate and maintain the inter-family discussions. Because of the nature of the problem, many of these discussions happened in multi-parent groups without the children present.

Because Mohammed had become very stuck both with his parents and with the teacher-therapists, the use of cross-family linkage was extremely useful in helping everyone experiment with new communication styles and behaviours. Mohammed's behaviour tended to detour conflict between his parents so that their attention was diverted from their marital conflict onto a parental concern for their son. Sameira, in particular, oscillated between being very angry but ineffectual with Mohammed and being overly protective and unable to tolerate any negative comment about her son's behaviour. When she eventually allowed Mohammed to work with another parent, she was amazed to see how competent he could be and how he did not use the same behaviours as he usually did with her. This other parent was not triggered by the feelings of guilt and anxiety which tended to organize Sameira's relationship with Mohammed and was able to set clear expectations of how they could communicate with each other. At the same time, Sameira worked with another boy and was able to experience herself as being confident and successful in developing a good relationship with him. For both Sameira and Mohammed, the chance to observe the other's different behaviours was pivotal in helping them to make changes in their relationship with each other.

Confidence gained from the cross-linkage activities enabled them to try to work together again, this time using their new behaviours. Sameira was praised and encouraged by the parental-support group. Other children gave Mohammed positive feedback when they saw him do something different. Most importantly, his schoolteachers noticed the difference and commented on it both directly and via the target sheets.

With new patterns of communication available, it was possible to talk about what formerly had been too anxiety-provoking to mention—a possible divorce. Aziz and Sameira were able to talk about ways of moving on and to plan an agreed separation. Once the separation had physically taken place and Aziz had moved into a place of his own, Mohammed and his brother were able to have a regular contact with their father that was uncontaminated by the acrimony and tensions that had defined the family relationships when they were all living together. Each parent could start to relax in the negotiations with the children without always being preoccupied with the unrelenting marital disputes. In turn, the children also started to calm down, and Mohammed in particular became less anxious and fearful about the future. Being the eldest, it appeared as if he had carried the greatest burden of worries about his family's unhappiness. As a result of the dramatic reduction in family tension, he rapidly became a much more sociable and confident boy. His behaviour at school subsequently improved remarkably, which enabled him to make significant and rapid progress in all areas of his learning.

Within the multi-family setting of the Family School there is plenty of scope for work with individual families as well as with individual family members. Moreover, there are also lots of connections made with the teachers in the local schools, focusing on the individual pupils, all of which has been comprehensively described elsewhere (Dawson & McHugh, 2000). However, it is our belief that the single most important ingredient of the success of the Family School is its multi-family work.

CHAPTER FIVE

Applications of
the Marlborough model

Over the years, many colleagues from different countries and work settings have visited the Marlborough's Family Day Unit and Family School. The day and residential units set up in the 1980s and early 1990s and in part inspired by our work, mostly located in Scandinavia, seemed to differ in two major aspects: the degree of inter-family work and the staffing levels. In these units, families largely tend to receive their therapeutic inputs separately, with only very occasional meetings involving other families. The therapeutic potential of families consulting to each other is not exploited, with all therapy provided only by staff. In some instances, the staff in residential family-units by far outnumber clients, with staff–client ratios of 3:1. How do families and their individual members construct the apparent need for such large staff numbers? Perhaps some might think that their problems are so serious that only multiple staff can have a hope of addressing these. Others will have their own sense of helplessness reinforced by the presence of too many helpers. Families and their individual members will tend to look to therapists to provide solutions for their problems and issues, to be addressed in formal therapeutic sessions. Conversely, in such settings therapists have to think of themselves as providing their special expertise, and these efforts can inadvertently lead to the "institutionaliza-tion" of their clients. It is at times quite difficult to understand what staff employed in large numbers do all day. One experience that the Marlborough team has had over and over again is how "unemployed" therapists can frequently feel in day or residential settings—even when it is only three of them dealing with up to ten families. If therapists see themselves predominantly as catalysts, enabling inter-actions between family members and families to take place, then this different frame can result in therapists being less central.

It may be of interest to list some of the reasons not infrequently put forward to explain why multi-family work could simply not be carried out in a specific unit. The issue of confidentiality is most commonly raised, as many staff believe—particularly when a day or residential family unit is located in a closely knit community—that it would not be possible for families to share private matters with other families, as "everybody knows everybody". There are understandable anxieties that families could become the victims of some vicious gossip, with the risk of further marginalization and social isolation. Our experiences in London, with families from very specific and well-circumscribed localities attending together, have shown that such fears are largely unwarranted. In fact, quite the reverse is the case: families tend to form friendships which survive their joint admission to our Family School or Family Day Unit. Many of the families form a social network, including setting up informal self-help groups locally, to provide similar help for other families in the neighbourhood. To almost all families, it comes as an enormous relief to discover that sharing personal or even "secret" information with fellow sufferers is a relief (Schuff & Asen, 1996). Staff need to give reassurances that it is up to each family to decide what can and what cannot be shared. At times, staff may feel a wish to protect individuals from disclosing certain painful information to a large group of families. This can be appro-priate, though it is, in the final analysis, a question of timing as to when certain information can be shared. A rigid protective stance carries the risk of inhibiting sharing, with a strong possibility of reinforcing the parents' beliefs that it is best to never talk about anything sensitive or anything that could be potentially embarrassing. In residential or day setting where multi-family work is carried out, there is always the need for some private space for individual family members. Individual conversations between family members and staff may therefore need to be scheduled, to explore fears and hopes of talking about personal issues—prior to doing so in the large group.

Another resistance to undertaking multi-family work has to do with fears of not being able to control large groups of families, or for things to spiral out of control, resulting in major crises and dangerous situations. While it has to be acknowledged that working with a number of potentially highly explosive families can be quite challenging, our own experiences have been positive. In twenty-five years and with more than a thousand families being part of our various multi-family programmes, we have not had a single crisis that resulted in anyone getting hurt.

The reason for this outcome is, of course, obvious: we get families to manage their crises themselves rather than setting ourselves up as being responsible experts in crisis management. The most frequent intervention during crises times is simple—the therapist asks: "What can *you* all now do to sort things out?" The emphasis is on getting families to identify their coping skills and to employ these usefully to resolve a crisis. What helps our staff is a sense of confidence—if not an at times delusional belief—that families have their own resources and coping skills which, if elicited, help them to manage any crisis. Staff communicate this belief effectively to families and this inevitably contributes to them getting actively involved and taking responsibility.

Different cultural and class backgrounds are other reasons cited to explain an apparent reluctance to undertake multi-family work. Language barriers can seem an obstacle, though by employing interpreters some of these can be overcome effectively. Ethnic and cultural differences are best addressed by exposing families from different backgrounds to one another, rather than by avoiding them. Over and over we have observed how prejudices and ignorance are best reduced when people become curious about their respective cultures and customs. This furthers tolerance and mutual understanding. Exchanges can take place at many different levels—from comparing notes about different child-rearing practices in various countries and exploring the possible reasons for these differences, to cooking meals for one another, exploring differences via taste buds and the stories that often get told in the kitchen about childhood memories around food and meals. The use of interpreters over long stretches of time may at the outset seem rather laborious and time-consuming. However, the very process of group discussions and interactions seemingly being slowed down, by waiting for both the translation to and from a particular language, in itself gets many families to become more tolerant and understanding of difference, creating hitherto unknown curiosity and interest in other cultures, customs, and social classes.

Lack of space is another common reason given for some units not being able to see a number of families simultaneously. Prior to their first visit to the Marlborough, many of our colleagues from different countries seem to be full of fantasies regarding the physical space available. Almost all of them are very "disappointed" to discover how small most of the rooms are. It is simply not necessary to have vast rooms. Multi-family work can be done with between three to eight families. The work as far as staff are concerned is much more exhausting if there are only two or three families present, as the inter-family interactions are more limited. While it is helpful to have specially designed day or residential units for multi-family work, it is also possible to use or adapt existing resources and to hire a room for specific multi-family activities. As described in other parts of this book, some of the work takes place outside—in a garden or park, for example.

It is our strong belief that most of the concepts used in the work of the Marlborough Family Day Unit and Family School can be transferred and adapted to other settings and, over the past ten years, this has happened in a number of different countries. What is even more encouraging is that new client groups have been targeted for multi-family work—for example, eating-disordered adolescents and their families.

Developing multi-family work
for eating-disordered adolescents

A number of projects, inspired by the experiences of the Marlborough model, involving eating-disordered adolescents are currently being piloted. Clinicians in Dresden and London are integrating these in multi-family programmes that extend over the course of a whole week. Preliminary results show that this approach is not only acceptable to patients and their families, but that there are also significant positive changes in the young persons' eating problems. These include improved recovery and reduced relapse rates, as well as changes in family dynamics.

The first experiment of applying multiple family therapy ideas to eating-disordered teenagers was pioneered in Dresden. The project started in 1998 in a busy child and adolescent psychiatry service that includes a supra-regional in- and outpatient service for eating-disordered adolescents. This service has, over the years, on average admitted about sixty anorectic and bulimic teenagers as inpatients, invariably in rather severe states, with most of them having already been treated by their local child and adolescent services. On the inpatient ward, a variety of simultaneous treatments and therapies was provided, ranging from behavioural interventions to individual psychodynamic and cognitive therapies, and occasional medication. Fortnightly family therapy sessions had been routine in all cases. The average duration of inpatient admission was in the region of three to six months. Once an adequate target weight had been achieved, the young person was discharged home and would usually continue to attend as a day- or outpatient, receiving individual and family therapy and, occasionally, medication.

A frequent observation made by the Dresden team was that, once discharged, patients tended to lose weight rapidly, particularly if the parents had not been involved in managing the eating routines and associated behaviours of their children. So-called successes regarding the teenagers' food intake and weight, achieved in the structured setting of the hospital ward, were almost inevitably not generalized to the home setting. The young persons tended to be readmitted within a few weeks, in similar states of emaciation. Dissatisfied with an ensuing revolving-door cycle, so common all over the world, the Dresden team questioned the wisdom of their approach: this seemed to be based on an intense, highly efficient ward regime implemented by experienced nurses, in strong contrast to the relatively low-intensity involvement if not exclusion of parents. It seemed obvious that parents had to be involved much more centrally, possibly right from the outset. Parents are not always welcome visitors on adolescent inpatient wards, particularly when staff believe, consciously or unconsciously, that the parents are to blame for the eating disorder of their child. There are doctors and nurses who think that the eating-disordered young person needs to be separated from her or his parents and that an inpatient admission would be extremely helpful to cut the umbilical cord and assist the young person to individuate. Parents also tend to be viewed by medical staff as interfering with the well–worked-out ward routines. Rivalries between staff and parents are not uncommon, particularly when it comes to who the "best" carer is, with the young person inevitably getting caught up in such dynamics. The frequently observed rapid weight loss following discharge from the inpatient unit only serves as confirmation that the hospital staff are "better" than the parents and further confirms the parents' failure. The parents feel increasingly demoralized and offer little resistance to their child's readmission to hospital, more keen to have her or him discharged later rather than sooner, with an ever-increasing risk of the young person becoming a chronic and institutionalized patient.

The multiple family therapy paradigm seemed highly relevant, since it addresses directly the parents' sense of struggling away in isolation and having to rely heavily on the input of nurses, doctors, and therapists. Connecting these parents with other parents seemed a logical step to overcome this isolation. Moreover, involving parents directly in the eating issues of their child seemed another step for them to become expert themselves rather than leave that expertise remaining with the nursing and medical staff. Food has multiple meanings in most families, and the failure to provide "goodness", "nourishment", "love", "affection", "care"—or to have these offerings rejected by one's child—inevitably releases powerful emotions.

Most parents with an anorectic child have a complex set of feelings—including failure, guilt, fear, and embarrassment—and so the opportunity to meet with other families who experience similar feelings allows for these to be shared. This has strong de-stigmatizing effects and creates a sense of solidarity. In a multi-family setting, professional staff are in a minority and this contributes to a "family" rather than "medical" atmosphere. Being in the presence of other families also has the effect of making the adolescents and their parents feel less central—they are part of a large group, and the feeling of being constantly watched and observed by staff is less intense.

The presence of other families highlights not only similarities but also differences between them, inviting comparisons. Families generally cannot help but become curious about one another—for example, how other parents handle the food-refusal of their teen-ager—just as much as young persons cannot help comparing their own parents' responses to those of other eating-disordered teen-agers. The effect of all this is that new and different perspectives are introduced, which is so important since many eating-disordered families tend to have distorted self-perceptions while being often very precise and intuitive about other families. Working alongside each other allows parents and teenagers to compare notes and learn from each other. Peer support and peer criticism are known to be powerful dynamics that can promote change. Many people find it easier to use feedback from fellow-sufferers than from staff—it seems more "credible" because these families all have painful di-rect experiences around food, hospitalization, and dieting. Such feedback gets generated during a whole range of different activities throughout the day, from joint meals, informal encounters, formal large-group discussions, creative-art work, or outings. The role of the therapist is that of a catalyst, enabling families to connect with one another and encouraging mutual curiosity and feedback.

In a multi-family setting, with very few staff present, families get the constant message that it is *their* job to deal with the eating and related issues. Such parental involvement can also be helpful to staff in that it can defuse or neutralize chronic staff–patient relationships. The battles that many anorectics are involved in for months when admitted to inpatient units often draw in staff, who re-enact behaviours and roles not dissimilar to those that the par-ents generally assume. Putting such teenagers into a multi-family context immediately transfers the conflicts to the family "front".

Instead of engaging in battles with staff, thus preserving the fantasy of a "nice" family, the young person has to confront her or his parents with the important issues, including eating, weight, and general conflict management.

We have explained elsewhere in this book that multi-family work permits the possibility of experimenting with surrogate parenting. Dealing, for short and well-defined periods, with the child of another family (or, conversely, with another parent)—"crossing over" as it were—may allow new experiences to take place. For example, an anorectic girl is likely to have different interactions with the mother of a fellow sufferer to those with her own mother. Moreover, this other mother may find it easier to have a conversation about a contentious issue with this girl rather than with her own daughter. Such an experience, witnessed not only by the two persons interacting but also by the "other" mother and daughter, tends to stimulate useful reflections about how things might develop differently if there were a bit more distance.

The day programme

Since its inception in 1998, the staff of the Dresden Eating Disorder Unit have experimented with a whole range of different lengths and frequencies of the programme (Scholz & Asen, 2001). It seems that the most appropriate package consists of an initial evening where up to eight families meet and hear about the proposed work from "graduated" ex-eating-disorder families. This is followed by an intensive week, consisting of five days and eight hours per day. One month later, families attend for two whole days—and this is repeated at monthly intervals. The whole multiple family therapy package takes, on average, nine months. The team is multidisciplinary, consisting of nurses, occupational therapists, teachers, social workers, psychotherapists, psychologists, and psychiatrists. The minimum staff for each multi-family group is four, with each professional having different functions and tasks, be that direct therapeutic work, observation, or supervision. The rooms are well equipped with video-cameras so that there is ample opportunity to record interactions, which can then be reviewed jointly by families and staff later that day or at some other suitable time.

The Dresden experiment has been carried out in parallel with a similar multi-family programme for eating-disordered teenagers, based in London at the Maudsley Hospital (Dare & Eisler, 2000). This was commenced in the spring of 1999 with a four-day block running from 9 a.m. to 5 p.m. Families subsequently attend for whole days, about monthly, for up to six months. There has been plenty of communication between the Dresden and London teams, and the overall approach as well as the programmed activities and timetable in both units are remarkably similar. Both programmes are very structured and require families and their individual members constantly to change context and to adapt to new demands. Such "heat" can simply not be created in individual family sessions. The sheer energy released in the course of such a programme provides a new "buzz" for adolescents and parents alike, and it creates hope. Such feelings of hope can be enhanced by mixing families who have gone through a multi-family programme with others who are new to it. When "old" families tell their story, this is frequently a considerable source of encouragement for the "new" ones, with a kind of preview of changes that might be possible for everyone.

Preliminary results show that the drop-out rate is very low in both centres. In many teenagers, there has been considerable somatic improvement (increased weight, return of menstruation, stabilization of eating, reduction of bingeing and vomiting, decreased laxative abuse). Family tension and dispute has been significantly reduced, and a cooperative and supportive atmosphere and working environment has been created for the young persons and their families. In Dresden, there has been a significant reduction in readmission rates.

The structure of each day is discussed and decided by the staff. The programme of a typical multi-family day is presented in Table 5.1. Families have an opportunity to discuss the programme for the day, and their ideas are often used to create a new structure for the day.

The programme is started by an introductory talk, given by a senior clinician, who explains the reasons for the work, both in terms of involving families in the treatment of their eating-

Table 5.1: Multi-Family Day

8:45	Weighing of each patient
9:00	Introductory talk and group discussion
9:30	Joint breakfast
10:00	Art work, genograms, body image
11:15	Reflective group
12:30	Joint family lunch
13:15	Informal time
13:45	Video feedback session
15:00	Reflective group
16:30	Tea and finish

disordered teenager, as well as providing a rationale for working with between six and eight families simultaneously. The introductory talk also contains a psycho-educational component, explaining the facts about eating disorders, their physical risks and psychological side effects, the role of the family, and societal trends. Following this introductory talk, families are encouraged to engage in open conversation with one another and exchange experiences, with "old" families also providing information about the work for "new" families. In Dresden, the clinicians have tried to mix old and new families, and there have been occasions when between forty and fifty people attended for the initial meeting, staff not included. Such a large group is a very specific context, providing hope for newcomers.

Breakfast is then served, providing an opportunity for studying family-interaction patterns around food. The next activity is designed by the occupational therapist. Parents and adolescents usually engage in parallel tasks, such as producing clay family sculpts, body-image work, or symbolic food preparation. In a subsequent multi-family session, each family presents their pieces of work to the group as a whole, with first the adolescent and then her or his parents explaining their respective works of art or the tasks undertaken. Other families are then encouraged to discuss their impres-

sions of this work and how it might relate to this particular famu,
issues. The ensuing discussions are usually stimulating all round,
thus providing ample opportunity for cross-family reflections.

Lunch is in many respects the central event of the day—at least
in the initial stages of multi-family work. In London, families go
shopping to the local supermarket, and here major confrontations
often ensue between the teenager and her or his parents as to what
is nutritious food. Once the food has been bought, families are in
charge of preparing and serving it. The situation is different in
Dresden, where food is provided by the hospital, with a fixed
menu within which there are a few choices. Each family decides
what and how much their daughter or son should eat. Needless to
say, soon familiar battles will flare up, with the anorectic making
out the best possible arguments for not eating anything, and the
parents determined to impose their will. The staff's role is to comment on and, if appropriate, challenge these interactions around
food "*in vivo*" and to question the parents' tolerance and their
willingness to compromise. Much of this is videotaped so that
parent–child interactions can be viewed and analysed in subsequent video-feedback sessions.

Lunch is followed by a thirty-minute "break", an informal time
when families are encouraged to meet with and talk to members of
other families. The subsequent video-feedback session aims at reviewing the day's key situations for each family, enlisting other
families to comment on what they themselves observe. This slot is
also used to ask experienced nurses to give a seminar on "Games
That Anorectics and Bulimics Play". Here, videotapes of recent
family interactions, particularly around eating, are shown to illustrate how eating-disordered teenagers attempt to deceive their
parents. This has proved to be a particularly popular slot with
parents, though much less so as far as the teenagers are concerned.

The final event of the day is a reflective group, when families
and staff alike reflect on specific and general aspects of the day's
work. Parents and adolescents exchange ideas and make plans for
the immediate future. The tea-time afterwards provides ample opportunity for families to have informal conversations or to make
plans for meeting outside the programme.

To date, about a hundred eating-disordered young persons
and their families have been seen in the multi-family settings in

Dresden and London. Preliminary results point to the clinical use-fulness of the approach, and formal studies and trials are now on the way. In common with other multi-family work is the surprisingly high acceptability of this form of therapy as far as family members are concerned. Generally, the drop-out rates are very low, with family tension and disputes being significantly reduced and consistent positive reports of this work creating a supportive atmosphere.

More recently a team at the Royal Free Hospital in London, led by Dr Paul Robinson, has adapted some of these ideas to their work with adult eating-disordered patients and their families (Colahan & Robinson, in press). The initial design of the programme consists of three day-long sessions taking place over a period of six weeks, with a half-day follow-up three months later. Each day includes a verbal element (discussion groups) and some experimental work (art, movement, and sculpting). Ratings made by participants indicate that families view the treatment very favourably, and patients appear to benefit substantially.

Mental Health Matters workshops

Another multi-family project that gained significant inspiration from the Marlborough model was set up in London over ten years ago—the "Family Matters" workshops, now renamed "Mental Health Matters" workshops (Bishop, Clilverd, Cooklin, & Hunt, in press). The family project team and associates consists of a number of professionals, including two half-time family therapists, together with a small contribution from himself, as well as from three consultant psychiatrists. The project had a brief to introduce family work into the regular professional practice of mental health services in a central London district. The focus of the project had initially been on training multidisciplinary groups of staff to "work with" the families of the patients in their care. The team had experienced frustration in achieving a genuine "climate-change" in the attitudes of the staff (some 1,200) as a whole. Following the publication of McFarlane's outcome trials in New York and Maine (McFarlane, 1990; McFarlane, Link, Dushay, Marchal, & Crilly,

1995), which compared multi-family with "single-family" group work, for families in which one member had suffered a psychotic episode, the team decided to try to replicate the approach. However, McFarlane's work had required considerable resources, including inpatient admissions and other responsibilities for all aspects of the patient's treatment. The resource implications far exceeded what was possible in that publicly funded provider unit at that time. Thus, as an alternative to confronting what seemed like insurmountable obstacles, the family project team in London started running single-day workshops for families that included a member who had suffered an episode of major mental illness. The format of the workshops was very similar to the preparatory evening and first day of the eating-disorder programme in Dresden, as described above—except that the workshops were explicitly defined as *not* being a form of treatment. Instead, they were presented as one-off educational events, available to patients and their families. However, the form and focus of the education included broader issues related to family relationships; the need for reciprocity in those relationships; advocacy in dealing with the frustrations associated with the mental health and other services, as well as more "formal" information about the meaning of diagnoses, the effects of both prescribed and non-prescribed drugs, the effects of alcohol, and so forth. As noted before, these meetings were soon renamed "Mental Health Matters" workshops, in recognition of the broader definition of "family" which was needed for this population, so as to include "surrogate" relatives—partners, friends, and carers. Although each workshop was designed as a "one-off" event, they were repeated on average every six weeks. Thus, a regular clientele developed, with a steering group that included both patients and relatives. A most interesting and rather unexpected finding to the staff group—which had grown from the actual family project workers to include increasing numbers of interested mental health professionals within the provider unit— was that the explicit definition of the groups as non-therapeutic seemed to be associated with a view, expressed by both patients and relatives, that the groups had been "the most helpful thing" that they had experienced during their involvement with the provider unit and hospital. Descriptions included reports of a "new understanding" about the illness; "the first help I have ever had with medication"; "the first time my family has had any help". There were also many statements, made by both patients and relatives, emphasizing the broader benefits of "feeling less alone".

Each workshop was designed with a particular theme, such as diagnosis, drug treatment, alternative therapies, "voices" groups, impacts of mental illness and hospital admissions on children, and so on. A workshop typically starts with a brief lecture, followed by a chaired question-and-discussion session. This is followed by small-group discussions (about 8–10 participants) which are topic-based—usually some theme related to the initial presentation of the day. Suggestions for a topic could also be taken from the ensuing discussion. A "reflections" plenary follows, concluding with a structured "feedback" ritual. The latter is organized by distributing cards. Participants are asked to write on a card any aspect of the workshop which they would like "more of" or "less of", as well as making "new suggestions". Each card is then placed into one of three pouches, labelled accordingly. The whole workshop of staff and participants then shares lunch, which is usually provided by an outside sponsor. This is followed by an additional lecture/demonstration and/or small-group discussion, followed in turn by a closing plenary with a discussion of future workshops or future suggested events. In the small groups, patients and their relatives are encouraged—not coerced—to join different groups, in order to foster the potential for "cross-family" and "cross-generational" relationships.

These workshops may include up to sixty to seventy participants, representing twenty to thirty families. They tend to develop both a culture and an energy of their own that far exceeds their rather modest original goals. Out of these have developed other related workshops—for example, for children and their parents in families in which one or more of the adults has suffered a major mental illness. The striking feature of this almost serendipitous evolution is that these workshops appear to have developed their own therapeutic potential, despite the family project team's explicit and stated intention that they should not be defined as a form of therapy. They also seem to have a powerful educational impact on the staff, who are encouraged to attend when patients for whom they are responsible participate.

As may have been noted by the reader, there has been no discussion about whether the workshops are based on a "psycho-educational" or a "systemic" model. The explicit aim is educational, in its broadest sense, and the reader must draw his or her own conclusions regarding the possible systemic potential of the workshops, as described (Alan Cooklin, personal communication).

Outlook

The recent successful application of multi-family work to different groups of patients and their families—including anorectic teenagers and adults, as well as persons diagnosed with major psychiatric illness—is an example how the ingredients contained in the Marlborough model can be modified and adapted. Other recent applications include work with children with brittle diabetes and compliance problems, with elderly psychiatric patients and their carers, and with families whose children present with chronic disabilities.

CHAPTER SIX

Skills and techniques in multiple family therapy

This chapter lists a variety of techniques and interventions that can be used in multiple family therapy. The context within which this work takes place as well the specific issues will dictate how the techniques are adapted or modified. Clearly, one of the key features of family group work is that it focuses on the whole group and the interactions between families rather than simply on one individual family. The therapists' stances are multi-positional: they join and disengage within short time-frames, and they are at different times central or peripheral to the group, always aiming to facilitate interactions between families.

Setting up multi-family groups

There are many different sizes of multi-family groups, ranging from three to sixteen or more families. Too few families, and the work is more difficult, with too few inter-family interactions and too much reliance on the therapist generating ideas. Families also tend to feel quite exposed in a small group. At the other end of the spectrum, too many families being seen at the same time carries the danger of therapists relying on the families to treat each other, losing sight of individual families and their members. Our favoured number of families is between six and eight. This does not require a similar number of therapists: each therapist should be able to be the key worker for up to three families at the same time. It is worth noting that units that have tried a much higher staff–patient ratio have found that their personnel often felt unemployed, not knowing what to do or else becoming too involved.

This approach tends to work best when families with similar issues are brought together, be it child abuse, serious school problems, eating disorder, diabetes, or other chronic illness. Differences in class, ethnicity, or age do not appear to be significant obstacles to the functioning of such groups. Families from quite diverse backgrounds can mix and create a context of mutual learning. Interpreters can be used with families whose first language is not English, and this enables families from other cultures to access relevant services. It also helps families from the dominant culture to become curious and more accepting of difference.

There are a number of contraindications to multiple family work. One of these has to do with the families' own reluctance. There are families who are simply not willing to attend simultaneously with others. Issues to do with privacy, confidentiality, or mistrust are the reasons most commonly given. While this may be challenged by therapists, in the end the families' wishes have to be respected. However, there are times when the therapists' own uncertainties or lack of skills may well feed into the families' perceived reluctance. In such instances, it is not surprising that families will tend to be even more resistant to suggestions that they deal with their issues in front of other families. There is one group of families—namely, those containing a known or suspected paedophile—where careful consideration needs to be given as to whether to include them in a multi-family programme. Awareness that there are paedophiles who target vulnerable women with children may well lead therapists to exclude these men from multi-family work because of the risk they pose to their own children as well as to those of other families.

Multi-family work can be carried out both in open groups and in closed groups. One advantage of working in open groups is that current members are able to let newcomers know about the culture of the group work, its benefits and difficulties. This often helps to engage families who may be anxious about attending a therapeutic group. Their peers can tell them about the nature of the work from the perspective of a user, which is likely to be quite different from that offered by staff. A disadvantage of open groups is their ever-changing composition. This can require that the therapists continually reappraise their own roles and positions when the demands being made by the new members are very different from those of the more experienced families. One major advantage of a closed group is that it can seem a safer setting, allowing for more personal disclosure and interchanges. It also allows the group to establish its own rules about communication and interaction, not unlike those that families develop over time, facilitating detailed exploration of patterns within and between families. A disadvantage of closed groups is that their own processes are at risk of becoming institutionalized at the expense of potentially useful unpredictability. This is a danger well documented by clinicians working in traditional therapeutic communities.

Some multiple family therapy focuses on a symptomatic individual whereas other work involves whole families who have become defined as dysfunctional or multi-problematic. In the latter case, it is quite likely that families will be under considerable pressure from professionals—usually social workers—for everyone to attend. For the families with a symptomatic member, it is often more difficult to convince all family members of their need to participate. It may take a series of meetings with different family members, prior to their joining the group, to achieve that goal. Inviting family members to visit and observe the group work without having to make any commitments themselves, leading to informal conversations with group members, can be a particularly useful way of engaging reluctant or sceptical relatives. The definition of who is a family member is left for the family to decide and need not be restricted to conventional notions.

A major aim in multi-family work is to create a supportive, yet challenging, goal-directed group. At the outset, it is the therapist's responsibility to explain the purpose and nature of the work envisaged. This can take the form of an informal talk or a more formal lecture containing psycho-educational components. In work with eating-disordered teenagers, for example, the effects of starvation on body and mind, the role of the family in the recovery, and the potential benefit of families working together can be described in an initial presentation. After the formal or informal talk, some time should be allocated for discussion so that families can reflect, raise questions, or comment on the various points.

The position of the therapist

Minuchin and Fishman (1981) comment on how, when working with a single family, the therapist's actual position in the room affects the process of therapy. The demands made on therapists when working with more than one family at the same time are more complex, as there are more possibilities available for intervention. With a number of families present in the same room, all possibly at different stages of their therapy and with different preoccupations, therapists need to be able continually to shift positions. Physical movement around the room, temporarily engaging with one family, orbiting around another, being in a distant-observer position to a third, all this is done with the aim of facilitating intra- and inter-family connections. In strong contrast to the sedentary model of delivering single-family therapy, a therapist working with a number of families should feel comfortable with being mobile. Therapists in multi-family work constantly reposition themselves, both physically and metaphorically, not just in relation to a specific family, but to the group as a whole.

Achieving some proximity and then rapidly disengaging (Stevens, Garriga, & Epstein, 1983) allows "on-the-hoof interventions"—therapeutic manoeuvres that arise from small concrete interactions in informal situations. For example, the therapist may only make brief contact with a family or individual members, possibly with the mother while she has a cigarette in the garden, possibly with the father as he struggles to get a meal together in the kitchen. The therapist may comment on issues of teamwork, or on the different responsibilities each partner has, inviting brief conversations which may be taken up later in the large-group setting. This is quite different from many single-family therapy sessions, in which a specific issue may be explored in depth, such as family history or specific dynamics. In multi-family work, the therapist can be thought of as a chemical catalyst, making more and new interactions possible, or at times causing perturbations to the family and the larger group.

The different time-scale over which multi-family groups operate affects the position and actions of the therapists. Work goes on over a number of hours or even a whole day and is therefore intense at one level. At another, it is diluted, given that it is shared out between a number of families. There is less pressure on the therapist to make the "perfect" intervention because there are so many more opportunities for therapeutic comment than in single-family therapy sessions. The informality of multi-family work is also one of its main strengths. Given that the work takes place in multiple contexts over an extended period of time, there is always another chance—whether on the underground, in the street, in the supermarket, or in the home.

There is a good reason for actively seeing families in a whole variety of different contexts. One way of approaching their presenting problems is to ask families when and where they encounter their specific difficulties. It is not uncommon, for example, for parents to say that they find it particularly difficult to control their small and unruly children when crossing busy roads, walking on pavements, or negotiating the underground. Others might find it more difficult to manage themselves or their children in cafés, supermarkets, or schools, and this is where issues often get enacted (Minuchin, 1974). Taking a group of families into a variety of different public and private settings is experienced by them as being less threatening, since there is safety in numbers, while feelings of isolation are reduced. Families feel less vulnerable to the usual disapproving glares or critical comments that often come from members of the public.

At the beginning of multi-family group work, the therapist is likely to assume quite an active stance, at times even attempting to regulate interactions between families. For example, the therapist can minimize potentially conflictual interaction between two sets of parents by channelling all the communications through the therapist.

Early on, or at a later stage if families need to feel confident about one another, the therapist will encourage one family to talk directly to another about a sensitive issue. The therapist will attempt not to be central in this interaction and will avoid either siding with one family against another or becoming triangulated.

Another position that the therapist may assume in relation to the large group is to comment on themes common to a number of families. These include children not listening, violence in the home, drug abuse, absent fathers, the impact of illness on families—the list is endless. In this situation, the therapist first frames the themes and only subsequently encourages families to talk to one another (see Figure 6.1).

Another position that the therapist can assume is designed to reinforce or expand information between families. This aims to block redundant patterns, challenge beliefs, and control the intensity of the interactions.

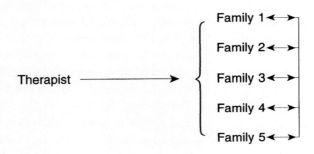

FIGURE 6.1

Techniques and examples
of multi-family group work

This section describes events, games, and tasks that can be used in multi-family group work. Many of these activities are action-oriented and are accompanied or followed by a process of reflection, inviting all families and their individual members to make sense of these events and what actually happened. This includes thinking about how these experiences might inform each person's future behaviour and actions. These feedback meetings require some organization and structuring so that all members of the family, including small children, can contribute. Given the often considerable age ranges of the individual members of multi-family groups, the language has to be comprehensible to everyone.

One of the major advantages of running task-based multi-family groups is that they allow people to try out new behaviours and ideas. To participate in such tasks as a single family in front of an observing therapist would be embarrassing and inhibiting. Defining a specific activity as a game in which a number of families get involved creates a context that facilitates playful and experimental behaviours. At times, a group setting can be much more conducive to overcoming natural inhibitions and can thus facilitate learning. Given that many of the adults will not have experienced play for many years if not decades, the reintroduction of playfulness can create possibilities for emotional connections that might have seemed lost forever.

The choice of multi-family activities depends on a number of factors: the ages and life-cycle stages of children and adults, their culture and ethnicity, the specific issues they want to address, the legal framework, and other contextual matters.

Outings

Rationale.   Many families experience some of their difficulties in public places. It may be embarrassing to go shopping when their children are out of control, resulting in the parents losing their own self-control. Searching out such situations provides the opportunity to study "*in vivo*" what happens and to find new coping mechanisms. Such an outing might be experienced as being quite threatening if it involved only one family and staff "observing". The context is very different when three or four families go together on such expeditions.

Technique

Prior to the outing, family members discuss scenarios that they are likely to encounter when going out. They are invited to comment on each other's strategies and make suggestions. Families are encouraged to identify potential crisis points and consider new responses so that different outcomes are likely. The possibility of filming the outing with a small camcorder is discussed. Different possibilities for outings are discussed—these include supermarkets, parks, museums, a zoo, or one of the families' homes. Many of the outings involve travelling on public transport (underground, bus), which is often experienced as very stressful for the families.

The staff's position is as that of an observing team which will, occasionally, get the family to reflect on whether they have achieved the target they set for themselves. Other families have the role of a "Greek chorus", providing a commentary on some of the actions of each family in turn.

Comment.   Many families find it helpful to deal in practical ways with everyday situations of stress. It gives them a sense that their "live" issues are being taken seriously and tackled there and then—namely, where they experience their difficulties. If the outing has been filmed with a hand-held camera, a video-feedback session some time later, with all families acting as consultants, is often a highly empowering experience for all concerned.

Preparation of joint meals

Rationale.   Meals are not only an important focal point but also a time of major conflict for most families. Parents can be angered and depressed when children fail to appreciate food that has been lovingly prepared. Mutual observation, support, and experimentation with different ways of handling familiar crises are best under-taken when there is more than one family present. For example, a parent can observe how others manage their unruly children while sweating over a hot stove. Prior to the advent of fast food and microwaves, the preparation of the family meal was a special time: in some cultures, it still is. Story-telling in particular has thrived in such situations. Involving a number of parents and children in planning and preparing a joint meal can evoke old times, thinking back to how meals were handled in the families of origin as well as in other cultures. Creating a "culture" of story-telling while the food is being prepared, with different parents exchanging stories from their childhood or their specific background, addresses issues of difference and ethnicity. For example, it is possible to encourage families from Africa, the Caribbean, and different parts of Asia to educate other families about culinary delights and eating habits, inviting curiosity and tolerance.

Technique

There are essentially two scenarios: either each of the families cooking their own meal or cooking used as a communal activity. In the second scenario families are asked to plan a joint meal two or three days ahead. They are encouraged to think about their own home or ethnic background and to incorporate this somehow into the meal.

On other days, it may be useful to get each family to prepare their own meals, and to encourage other families to become curious about one another during the preparation, the serving of it, the actual meal, and the subsequent clearing up.

It is also possible to stage metaphorical meals, particularly with families who have an eating-disordered member. Here, parents and children, in separate rooms, cut out from food magazines images of food and stick them on to real plates. The parents may, for example, prepare the "ideal" Sunday lunch for their offspring, while the children, in a separate group, may also prepare metaphorical meals, by cutting out similar images, speculating about the sort of meal that their parents might wish to prepare for them for Sunday lunch. In a multi-family setting, each family compares parental and child collages in public, discussing similarities and differences.

It is also possible to invert roles and ask, in a role-play, for the children to be concerned adults—and for the parents to be eating-disordered. In some role-plays, the children make the parents eat what they have served, with the parents acting the reluctant eating-disordered teenager.

Comment. The actual consumption of food is of specific interest in families containing eating-disordered adults or children. Minuchin and his team have described the "lunchtime session" (Minuchin, Rosman, & Baker, 1978), and while one is impressed by the enormous potential for change during such enactments, there often remains some discomfort regarding the coercive elements of this approach. It is possible to avoid this aspect of lunchtime sessions by seating three families per table, thus allowing them to watch one another and—eventually –to verbalize these observations. The therapist's task is not, as in Minuchin's model, to support the parents to support each other to "make" the young person eat the amount and type of food they have decided upon. Instead, the therapists see it as their job to highlight the impasse ("I can see you don't want to eat this . . . and I can see that your parents want you to carry on, but not wholeheartedly . . . they seem a bit undecided . . . What would help you, Mr and Mrs Smith, to move on? Maybe you want to discuss that with Mrs and Mrs Miller here, next to you . . ."). Involving other families in the internal monologues or dialogues of one's own family is a potentially fruitful cross-linkage.

Home occasions

Rationale. Socially isolated families tend to reinforce their isolation by never inviting anyone to visit their home. They may feel ashamed to have their children's friends inspect what they regard as their humble surroundings, and this sense of shame often increases as time goes on. Letting anyone into one's private space may become a major block. In a multi-family setting, it is possible to experiment with reversing this trend. Families can use one another to rehearse inviting someone to the house, including giving a small party.

Technique

One family plans a tea party, a birthday party, or a meal for friends. Other families will help them to think about how to plan, prepare, and budget. Once rehearsed, the event takes place a few days later, with two or three families attending, and they give feedback on the experience.

Comment.   Bringing three or more families to the house and doing this in a context where mutual feedback is the "culture" helps to prepare for "real life".

Control and power games

Rationale.   Many of the families attending the Family Day Unit present with problems that they themselves or professionals have defined as "control issues". The parents usually perceive their child as too powerful, and they feel utterly controlled by him or her. However, professionals—usually social workers—are involved in these families because the perceived "lack of control" of the parents has resulted in child abuse or neglect. In such situations, characteristically parents define their children as "abusive" whereas the social system calls the parents "abusive". Addressing issues of control therefore seems highly relevant, and this can be done through a number of games.

Technique

Tug of war is such an activity. All the children, however small, line up on one end of a rope, all the adults on the other. Each side is encouraged to pull as hard as possible. It is not uncommon in the first round of this activity for the adults to allow the children to "win". When asked why and how they decided this, answers usually include "it's good for children to win". This theme is then taken up by staff, who ask when it is appropriate for children to "win" and when it might be more appropriate for parents to do so. The resulting discussions are inevitably rich and varied. The adults are then encouraged to plan what is going to happen in the second round. Almost always they decide that it is their turn to "win". This creates a lot of turbulence among the children, who definitely want to "win" the third round. This then raises issues about "giving in", and soon debates emerge as to how serious one should be when playing games, when it is right for parents to win, and when children have to accept that they need to "lose"—that is, obey!

Doormat is a game that involves all the parents lying down on the floor, and the children using them as "doormats". It is up to each parent to negotiate with their own children how much their children are allowed to trample on them. The parents are also encouraged to tell the children about the consequences if things get "out of control". This game usually starts in good humour but can get quickly out of hand, enabling everyone to see how control issues are being handled. Again, families are encouraged to "compare notes".

Controlling children/undisciplined parents is another game that addresses control issues. The children are told that for the next ten minutes they should behave as if they were the parents of some very naughty children and that their task is to make them listen. The parents are told that they have to act like really naughty children. The role inversion leads to lively scenes, which are followed by reflection. It is always surprising for parents to see how children in role use all the techniques and tactics that they themselves have used. This communicates to the parents that the children have been listening to their parents in the past, and that lack of discipline is not a result of children being "deaf" but, rather, an indication that they simply do not wish to put into practice what they are being told. During a subsequent meeting, parents may reflect about their own contribution to their children's undisciplined behaviour.

In *role reversal*, families are divided into paired working groups. Family A is given the task of observer/ideas-generator. Family B is asked to reverse roles. The children are to sit on chairs, the parents on the floor. A number of pencils, videos out of their cases, and toys are spread on the floor. The children in Family B are told that they are now pretending to be the parent, and they have the job of persuading their child to tidy up.

As the child struggles with this task, Family A are asked to make notes of the strategies used and give them marks out of 10 on effectiveness. Family A are allowed to stop the action three times to make suggestions, but they are not allowed to take over. This task can last for fifteen minutes. The families then change over, and the task is repeated.

The multi-family group reassembles, and in the feedback Family A describes what they observed of Family B. Children can talk about what it is like being a parent. Parents can say what felt like "effective parenting" and what didn't work.

The group can draw up a checklist of reminders for sympathetic parenting, such as:

> In disciplining your child have you
> - Listened to your child's point of view?
> - Managed not to go overboard because you were worried?
> - Made sure you were clear about your expectations?
> - Given clear directions, using language your child understands?
> - Managed not to shout?
>
> and so on.

Comment. The main therapeutic opportunity lies in the cross-family feedback. Insightful observations by children about how parents fail should be valued. Sometimes a parent may find the task difficult, as it requires the capacity to play and to abandon the security of the authority role. In such cases, we have found that it is important to work at that adult's pace. By allowing such an adult to have a longer time in the observer role and by decreasing the active time sequences, the most reluctant parent can be persuaded to participate. It is more important that such parents join in the thinking than play on the floor.

Family painting and sculpting

Rationale. Representing images of the family through art work permits different perspectives.

Technique

The task set to each family is to jointly paint a picture on a large whiteboard with felt pens, or, alternatively, on a huge piece of paper, allotting each person some space. Each family starts this on their own, and the process of creating the picture itself is of course of interest: who organizes the picture, who allocates space, who has most and least space, etc. Families can be given thirty minutes to complete a picture. The theme can be given: a family, a house, life next year, etc. Once all families have completed their picture, it is "exhibited" on the wall, just like in an art gallery.

An alternative task is to make a model of the family out of clay. If children are old enough to do this themselves, they can be encouraged to make one model while the parent(s) do their own. Again, these are exhibited, and the therapists ask each family or child to talk about or explain their sculpture. Alternatively, the parent may be asked to describe the child's sculpture and vice versa, or even to "interpret" why the figures might look like that, why they are in specific positions. This task lends itself to thinking about how different people in the same family see things differently. Once other families get involved, additional perspectives are introduced.

Working with collages is another way of creating family images that depict people's preoccupations and reveals different approaches to the task. Food magazines, travel brochures, teenage magazines, photographs, and other visual materials are provided by staff, and each family is asked to mount their own collage on a large piece of cardboard. There are many different themes that can be used for this activity, such as "family life next year" or "your worst fears."

The collages are exhibited so that families can comment and question.

Comment. For many parents, making things with their hands is something that they have not done for years. They often experience flash-backs to their childhoods, enabling them to tell their own stories.

"Circle Game"

Rationale. Many families regard themselves as outsiders, having been marginalized by society at large, and by their neighbourhoods or families in particular. Moreover, in families there are individuals who may find it difficult to break in to the inner circle. This game addresses issues of how to "get into things".

Technique

All families get together and form a giant circle. This circle protects a special space. The therapist explains that often people want to "get into" a special place (or group) but are too inhibited to do so or are actively prevented from doing so. The therapists asks everyone to hold on to each other and face to the outside. The therapist then says that he wants to get into the circle and that he will try anything to do so. He makes some attempts, but the group will be reluctant to let him in. The therapist then asks one family to join him or her so they can try together. This involves a discussion of tactics, such as tickling, distraction, and force. Each family will have their turn. It is possible to have a discussion, as the process goes on, about the different strategies that families and individuals adopt. The discussion can also take place later, using a videotape of the game.

This game can also be reversed as "letting out". A family is placed in the middle of the group and asked to leave. The other families are now facing inside.

Comment.   A popular activity, eliciting often moving narratives about exclusion.

"Desert Island"

Rationale.   This activity deals with crises: what do people do when there is a crisis, and how do they adapt their lives in the aftermath.

Technique

The therapist sets up the shape of a boat using chairs, paper, or whatever is to hand. He or she invites the families on board the luxury liner for a Caribbean cruise. As soon as everyone has relaxed in the sun, there is a call to abandon ship. Everyone is encouraged to get as rapidly as possible into the liner's single small lifeboat. In shark-infested waters, the families must discuss and decide who can go in the lifeboat and who must swim behind. The story can extend to landing on a desert island, where ideas are needed about finding water, food, and shelter. Will each family work within itself, or can cross-family cooperation develop? The game can be amplified and spun out in many directions.

Comment. The main issue is clearly how families adapt to rapid change, how they allocate roles, and how they implement decisions. There can be a group discussion afterwards, or a videotape analysis.

"Magic Forest"

Rationale. This is an activity that addresses issues of tenderness and caring.

Technique

Families are asked to build a magic forest by using ornaments, papier mâché, objects, etc. The therapist then explains that each family should choose some specific animals that they might want to "become" for a few minutes. These can be "tender" animals or "wild" animals, anything from a parrot to a tiger. Once each of them has decide which animal to be, they are asked to set up a scene and act in the role of their chosen animal. This could be in the form of, for example, taking care of one another, providing appropriate shelter, or fending off any potential intruders. Families are encouraged to keep this up for some fifteen minutes.

Comment. Often this is a novel experience, allowing tenderness in a playful situation when they are not "themselves" but in role. Families are encouraged to think about what they were able to do while in role and why they found this easier than in real life.

Keeping children safe

Rationale. Protecting children from harm is a serious concern for parents and professionals alike. Many schools have introduced child-protection programmes into their curriculum, often using specialist trainers from outside the school. These projects have been effective within the community of the school, but they rarely involve parents, who risk remaining isolated from them. Many parents increasingly feel excluded by the education authorities, who target their children with "approved" programmes. Parental attitudes and judgements as to what is safe vary enormously. By involving parents in the personal-safety training of their children, it is possible to explore how they themselves assess and address potential risk situations. For example, is it risky for a child to stay overnight at a friend's house or to go on a school trip? How does a parent assess safety without appearing too overprotective? How can children trust their instinctive feelings? How can they talk to adults when they feel at risk or unsure?

Technique 1

In preparation, parents watch any of the published child personal-safety training videos to promote initial discussion about risk situations and child-protection issues. These videos distinguish between "good" and "bad" touches and show a number of different scenarios, involving inappropriate sexual approaches between adults and children, including intra-family sexual abuse. The videotape is put on pause after each sequence, and parents are asked how they would handle their own children's questions around specific issues. They are encouraged to imagine their children's responses and how they might handle these. A few days later the video is shown to the parents together with the children, and inter- and intra-family discussions are encouraged.

Technique 2

A guided role-playing game can be used to promote personal-safety strategies. For example, a staff member in the role of a stranger pretends to be asleep in the corner of the room while the parents sit in a semicircle as observers. With the children sitting on the floor, another staff member starts to narrate the " let's pretend" story. It can start with:

> "One day a group of children were looking for somewhere to play. In the corner of the room they thought there was a bundle of old clothes left for the refuse collectors, until someone saw the bundle move."

Interactive questions begin with the children.

- What should the children do?
- Why?
- What would happen if . . . ?

The children can move into role as the children in the story. They are encouraged to try out the group suggestions. The stranger, in role, poses a number of dilemmas for the children by asking questions like: "Can you find me something to eat?" "My dog is sick and has run away—I need someone to help me find him. Can you help me?"

The storyteller constantly stops the action to ask what children or parents should do at that point and why. The story and questions are matched to the age and maturity of the group. The group of parents is allowed to stop the action using the word FREEZE and can pose their own question or suggestion.

At the end, the staff member working with the parents "de-roles" the children, by asking them to give their name, age, which parent they are with today, and one toy/object/person in their life that makes them feel safe.

The whole multi-family group then reassembles, and discussion takes place looking at:

- How do we sense danger: what happens with our bodies?
- What can we do if an adult's words are nice but we feel funny/wrong/scared/worried?
- How can we make ourselves safe?
- If this really happened, what should we do?
- What do we do if the adult gets angry?

Technique 3

This exercise can be repeated outside the therapy room. The group is given details of an outing to a public place. The families are also told that, at some point, a stranger (a member of staff not known to the children) will come and ask for their help. It is for the families to decide how to manage the situation. Parents should encourage children to take time to think about what the stranger is asking, how it makes them feel, and what choices they have.

Comment. Discussing issues of personal safety and how parents' own experiences organize their personal belief systems about keeping oneself safe may be distressing for some parents. Not infrequently, this results in a parent disclosing an abusive experience that they may not have talked about before. Sometimes it can be helpful to use a diagram of the human body to facilitate discussion about bodily reactions to stress and fear. Adolescents may prefer to talk about an external picture rather than describe their own bodies; smaller children can have fun deciding where the butterflies in the tummy come from.

Developing trust

Rationale. Families with multiple problems and multiple-agency involvement, under professional scrutiny for lengthy periods, not surprisingly find it difficult to feel that they can trust others. This may have the effect of worsening social isolation. To combat this, exercises can be designed to address the steps needed to repair relationships where trust has been eroded.

Technique 1

Each person is to pair up with someone from another family. A is asked to place his or her hand on the shoulder of B, or hold hands with B, who then closes his or her eyes. A then guides B around the room at a slow pace in silence.

A is then asked to quicken the pace to a faster walking speed. B is given the job of controlling the speed by calling out 1 for slow and 2 for faster. Nobody is allowed to run. The task is repeated with A and B reversing roles.

A and B are asked to talk for five minutes, to tell each other what they liked about being a leader and what they liked about being led. The exercise is repeated, but this time the leader gives a running commentary on the journey—e.g. " we are just passing a window and heading towards the door". Depending on the experience of the group, it is sometimes more fun to add some obstacles to the course.

A and B reverse roles again, and speed control is given to the person being led.

A and B are again encouraged to talk about their likes and dislikes in the being-led role. Each participant helps the other to put into words his or her communication preferences in a trust task.

The whole group is then given a few minutes to discuss their experiences of the trust exercise.

Technique 2

Each child faces away from his or her parent, standing as close together as they can. The parent takes half a step backwards. Each child raises his or her arms to shoulder height and stretches them out sideways. In his or her own time, the parent should encourage the child to fall back into his or her arms. When the child is comfortable with this exercise, the parent can step back another half step, increasing the distance and again encourage the child to fall back. The distance can continue to increase by negotiation.

The session can end with a group-trust exercise. All group members form a circle and gradually bend their knees so that each person gently sits on the knees of the person behind them, while supporting the person in front. If the group is successful, they should be able to form a perfect sitting, self-supporting circle.

Comment.   It is important to ensure that everyone has enough time to say which communications increase their trust, and to voice any resulting boost in confidence. These exercises are physical metaphors for trust, support, and cooperation. They can also bring fun and safe playfulness back into the family repertoire.

Posters

Rationale.   Feelings of disappointment of parents about their children and vice versa can turn to bitterness and result in constant mutual criticism. When families fail to notice children's attempts to be good, they can fall into unhelpful patterns in which behaviour, good or bad, is rewarded randomly. This can lead to children being on constant alert for parental approval. Alternatively, they can become disillusioned and revert to the kind of behaviours that will guarantee a parental reaction. Parents can feel under siege by seemingly ungrateful children, with accusations of uncaringness being made on both sides. Externalizing dreams of the idealized relationship by committing them to paper is a safe way of examining the gap between wishes and disappointment, and of challenging assumptions

Technique

Children and adults are invited separately to design posters. The child is asked to prepares a "Wanted" poster, describing their "ideal" parent. The adult prepares a poster advertising for an "ideal" child.

The participants are encouraged to list qualities that are potentially achievable. When the posters are completed, each person pins his or hers up on the wall and then talks about the poster, with the rest of the group listening and commenting.

Comment.   Staff may need to assist in the initial phase and help nervous participants to feel secure about committing their ideas to paper. While participants are feeding back ideas, staff act as time-keepers and positive interrupters of any negative feedback.

"The Good-Luck Chain"

Rationale.   Noticing something new or positive can be a major achievement for families that spend much of their time focusing on problems.

Technique

The group forms a circle, and one member prepares to throw a soft object to another across the circle. The thrower calls the name of the recipient, and the recipient calls out his or her favourite colour/food/TV programme. The object is then thrown with the words: "I want to wish you good luck. I've noticed that you have a much calmer voice today, which you didn't do before. Well done."

The recipient replies with a thank you and throws the object to someone else. The process is repeated until everyone has made a positive comment.

Comment. On occasions, a group member finds it quite impossible to say anything positive. This is noticed by the group, who then reflect on it and provide ideas to help with positive naming of changes.

Family photographs

Rationale. This activity is designed to address memories and loyalty issues in families.

Technique

Each family is asked to choose six photographs that are reminders of joyful moments in the past. In the group, they take turns to tell the story of their photographs. Each family has ten minutes. After the allotted time, other families are encouraged to ask questions and give feedback.

Comment. This task is particularly useful in families where there has been an attempt to protect children by a parent acting as if the past does not exist. An example might be a painful divorce or a significant death in the family. This retrieval of positive memories can be helpful for children's cognitive development; areas of thinking are enabled rather than disallowed. Following this work, parents can put their photographs into a book, with commentary, as a gift for their children.

Outlook

There is a seemingly endless number of possible exercises and games that can be used and invented in multi-family settings. Many of the examples above were developed on the spur of the moment, in collaboration with families, dramatizing particular issues that seemed to be around that day. Some of the games and exercises were then elaborated. Multi-family work is stimulating precisely because it is a context for cross-fertilization. Every day, new ideas emerge that groups take up in their own idiosyncratic ways, allowing individuals and families to discover new perspectives and ways of being with one another.

Epilogue

Steps towards
multiple family group therapy

At present, there are a few units in a number of different countries which have been specifically designed to carry out intensive multiple family therapy, usually with so-called multi-problem families. In order to implement such work, systemic therapists need to acquire specific skills and confidence. Visiting units that practise multiple family therapy may help to overcome natural fears that working simultaneously with more than one family would be extremely difficult if not impossible. Ironically, quite the reverse is the case. With a number of families in the same room, the therapist can be much more mobile, moving from one family to the next, with thinking time while on the move, in the knowledge that families also help one another. It may be salutary for systemic practitioners to recall their initial experiences of working with families, usually after having had some experience of working with individuals. The initially frightening thought of dealing with, say, four people rather than just one person in the consulting-room must be a familiar memory to many of our colleagues. Yet, many trained family therapists will now find it easier to deal with a family rather than an individual in therapy. A similar process does occur in the course of getting involved in multiple family work—much of it becomes easier once one has acquired the necessary skills as, after some initial prompting, families tend to interact with one another. They do much of the work themselves, with therapists often feeling quite redundant. It is an interesting observation that therapists involved in multi-family work often report that they "don't know what to do"—not because of a lack of skills but because this work carries a lot of its own momentum, rendering therapists at times redundant. In multi-family work, therapists are much less central, more in an observer position, acting mostly as catalysts, leaving the stage—and the direction—to families and their individual members. It is possible for two therapists, one in a more active and the other in a more reflective role, to run groups comprising up to twelve families!

Introducing multi-family work to one's work setting might be quite difficult. Colleagues are likely to be sceptical, and their resistance may take the form of saying that there is not an appropriate space to carry out such work; that it is an unproven method; that they do not possess the right skills; that it raises too many confidentiality issues; and so on. In response to these doubts, one can counter that it is possible to carry out multi-family work in small rooms and that it is also possible to rent a bigger room for a few multi-family events. Multi-family work has been evaluated with schizophrenic and anorectic patients as well as with multi-problem families and families containing a chronically ill person.

Multi-family work may initially be anxiety provoking, but it is above all exciting. It addresses chronic staff–patient relationships as it helps staff to see their clients and families through the lenses of other families. Similarly, "chronic" clients and families will see overfamiliar staff in a new light as they have to reposition themselves. With a number of families in the same room, therapists are much less central than in other forms of systemic therapy. They can afford to be mobile, moving from one family to the next, thinking while on the move, in the knowledge that there are plenty of "co-therapists", in the shape of the families and its members (Stevens et al., 1983). Families are consultants to other families; they are there to help one another.

The metaphor of the "Greek Chorus", once introduced by Papp (1980) to describe strategic manoeuvres of the therapeutic team, takes on an entirely different meaning when used to describe group processes in multi-family work. Here, the individual or the family—the protagonists—tell their story or en-act their issues, in front of a group of people—other families—who are then asked to comment. In the classical Greek tragedies of Aeschylus, the chorus was the preserver of the world order: it was through the chorus that the Gods spoke to the people. The chorus amplified and intensified the action on the stage, reflecting from different perspectives on what went on and inviting the spectators to join these reflections. The protagonists in these Greek dramas became increasingly less important—their individual stories of love and hate, of ambition and defeat, were put in a larger frame: that of general human suffering and joy. Seeing things in perspective, as well as seeing things from different perspectives, are major aims and outcomes in multi-family work. Theatre and play are aspects of the work: staged games, mini role-plays, sculpts, and film-making are but a few of the many dramatic techniques used.

Michael White's notion of the "outsider witness group" (White, 1997) can be used to provide another frame for conceptualizing the therapeutic potential of multi-family work. The individual's and families' stories about life, relationships, and identity are enriched by listening to the group's retellings of these stories. The "outsider witness group"—the other families in this case—adds to the person's and family's narrative resources by sharing experiences from other lives, triggered by listening to the story of the family in focus. It permits every group member the possibility to connect or resonate with what is being told, to shift focus subtly, thereby introducing nuances bit by bit. Through this process, multiple family therapy generates multiple new perspectives and experiences, thereby opening up a multiverse for new and curious enquiry.

The renewed interest in this type of work in recent years is promising, and this book has hopefully demonstrated how the early clinicians working with the multi-family paradigm have inspired the Marlborough team. The developing Marlborough model of working intensively with whole groups of families in diverse contexts has, in turn, inspired multiple teams in different countries, creating contexts for change.

Last word(s)

It is the families and their individual members who will have the last word(s). Over the years, we have attempted to evaluate what those who participate in multiple family group work make of it. Back in the 1980s, we commissioned a survey of families who had attended the Marlborough Family Day Unit (Cooklin et al., 1983). Three-quarters of the parents interviewed stated that they found that their attendance addressed their problems and that the sharing of their experiences with other families was "very helpful". A more recent study (Summer, 1998) has confirmed that families appreciate learning from one another and that, even in the context of serious child abuse, the sharing of painful experiences and the joint search for new solutions in a group setting feels less persecutory. In multi-family work with eating-disordered teenagers and their families (Scholz & Asen, 2001), it has been shown that all participating parents and 80% of teenagers regarded working together with other families jointly in a day-hospital setting as helpful and desirable.

Here then are some verbatim quotes of what families have said after participating in multiple family group therapy:

"Changes have happened by hard work, openness, and the support of others. It was great to know others with similar problems."

"In a group like this there is always someone to listen to you and give time."

"I felt we're all in the same boat together."

"We were able to see in other families what we couldn't see about our own family."

"I didn't like it that my parents talked to other parents about my eating problems . . . but they became more confident and I think it helped me in the end."

"I hated every minute of it, but I'd do it again."

"When you first come, you think you're the only person in the world suffering this problem and then you meet others in the same mess, you listen to them talking and then you see the light at the end of the tunnel."

"It felt like one big family . . . with all the good and bad bits."

REFERENCES

Andersen, T. (1987). The reflecting team. *Family Process, 26*: 415–428.

Anderson, C. M. (1983). A psychoeducational program for families of patients with schizophrenia. In: W. R. McFarlane (Ed.), *Family Therapy in Schizophrenia*. New York: Guilford.

Asen, K. E., George, E., Piper, R., & Stevens, A. (1989). A systems approach to child abuse: management and treatment issues. *Child Abuse & Neglect, 13*: 45–57.

Asen, K. E., Stein, R., Stevens, A., McHugh, B., Greenwood, J., & Cooklin, A. (1982). A day unit for families. *Journal of Family Therapy, 4*: 345–358.

Bateson, G. (1973). *Steps to an Ecology of Mind*. London & New York: Paladin.

Bishop, P., Clilverd, A., Cooklin, A., & Hunt, U. (in press). Mental health matters: a multi-family framework for mental health intervention. *Journal of Family Therapy*.

Cirillo, S., & DiBlasio, P. (1992). *Families That Abuse*. New York & London: W. W. Norton.

Colahan, M., & Robinson, P. (in press). Multi-family groups in the treatment of young adults with eating disorders. *Journal of Family Therapy*.

113

Cooklin, A. (1982). Change in here-and-now systems vs. systems over time. In: A. Bentovim, G. Gorell-Barnes, & A. Cooklin (Eds.), *Family Therapy: Complementary Frameworks of Theory and Practice*. London: Academic Press.

Cooklin, A., Miller, A., & McHugh, B. (1983). An institution for change: developing a family day unit. *Family Process, 22*: 453–468.

Dale, P. (1986). *Dangerous Families*. London: Tavistock Publications.

Dare, C., & Eisler, I. (2000). A multi-family group day treatment programme for adolescent eating disorder. *European Eating Disorders Review, 8*: 4–18.

Dawson, N., & McHugh, B. (1986a). Families as partners. *Pastoral Care in Education, 4* (2): 102–109.

Dawson, N., & McHugh, B. (1986b). Application of a family systems approach in an education unit. *Maladjustment and Therapeutic Education, 4* (2): 48–54.

Dawson, N., & McHugh, B. (1987). Talking to parents of children with emotional and behavioural difficulties. *British Journal of Special Education, 14* (3): 119–121.

Dawson, N., & McHugh, B. (1988). Claire doesn't talk: behavioural or learning difficulty. *Gnosis, 12*: 8–11.

Dawson, N., & McHugh, B. (1994). Parents and children: participants in change. In: E. Dowling & E. Osborne (Ed.), *The Family and the School: A Joint Systems Approach to Problems with Children*. London: Routledge.

Dawson, N., & McHugh, B. (2000). Family relationships, learning and teachers—keeping the connections. In: C. Watkins, C. Lodge, & R. Best (Eds.), *Tomorrow's Schools—Towards Integrity*. London: Routledge.

Dowling, E., & Taylor, D. (1989). The clinic goes to school: lessons learnt. *Maladjustment and Therapeutic Education, 7* (1): 24–31.

Evans, J. (1982). *Adolescent and Pre-adolescent Psychiatry*. London: Academic Press.

Ezriel, H. (1950). A psycho-analytic approach to group treatment. *British Journal of Medical Psychology, 23*: 59–74.

Goffman, E. (1961). *Asylums*. New York & London: Anchor Books.

Gonsalez, S., Steinglass, P., & Reiss, D. (1989). Putting the illness in its place: discussion groups for families with chronic medical illnesses. *Family Process, 28*: 69–87.

Harrow A. (1970). A nursing approach to multiple family group therapy. *Proceedings of 5th Conference A.P.S.A.* Edinburgh.

Jenkins, H., & Asen, K. E. (1992). Family therapy without the family: a framework for systemic practice. *Journal of Family Therapy, 14*: 1–14.

Jones, M. (1968). *Social Psychiatry in Practice.* London: Pelican Books.

Kanner, L. (1943). Autistic disturbances of affective contact. *Nerv. Child., 2*: 217–250.

Kaufman, E., & Kaufman, P. (1979). Multiple family therapy with drug abusers. In: E. Kaufman & P. Kaufman (Eds.), *Family Therapy of Drug and Alcohol Abuse.* New York: Gardner.

Kuipers, L., Leff, J., & Lam, D. (1992). *Family Work for Schizophrenia: A Practical Guide.* London: Gaskell.

Laing, R. D. (1960). *The Divided Self.* London: Tavistock Publications.

Laing, R. D., & Esterson, A. (1964). *Sanity, Madness, and the Family.* London: Tavistock Publications.

Lansky, M. R. (1981). Establishing a family oriented in-patient setting. In: G. Berenson & H. White (Eds.), *Annual Review of Psychotherapy, Vol. 1* (pp. 447–464). New York: Human Sciences Press.

Laqueur, H. P. (1972). Mechanisms of change in multiple family therapy. In: C. J. Sager & H. S. Kaplan (Eds.), *Progress in Group and Family Therapy.* New York: Brunner/Mazel.

Laqueur, H. P. (1973). Multiple family therapy: questions and answers. In: D. Bloch (Ed.), *Techniques of Family Psychotherapy.* New York: Grune & Stratton.

Laqueur, H. P., La Burt, H. A., & Morong, E. (1964). Multiple family therapy: further developments. *International Journal of Social Psychiatry, 10*: 69–80.

Leichter, E., & Schulman, G. L. (1974). Multiple family group therapy: a multidimensional approach. *Family Process, 13*: 95–110.

Mawson, A. B., & Meyer, R. (1972). Marlborough Day Hospital. *Lancet, i* (7765): 1402.

McFarlane, W. R. (1982). Multiple family in the psychiatric hospital. In: H. Harbin (Ed.), *The Psychiatric Hospital and the Family.* New York: Spectrum.

McFarlane, W. R. (1990). Multiple family groups and the treatment of schizophrenia. In M. I. Hertz, S. J. Keith, & J. P. Docherty (Eds.), *Handbook of Schizophrenia, Vol. 4: Psychosocial Treatment of Schizophrenia.* New York: Elsevier Science.

McFarlane, W. R. (Ed.) (1993). Multiple family groups and the treatment of schizophrenia. In: *Family Therapy in Schizophrenia*. New York: Guilford Press.

McFarlane, W. R., Link, B., Dushay, R., Marchal, J., & Crilly, J. (1995). Psychoeducational multiple family groups: four-year relapse outcome in schizophrenia. *Family Process, 34*: 127–144.

Minuchin, S. (1974). *Families and Family Therapy*. Cambridge, MA: Harvard University Press.

Minuchin, S., & Fishman, C. H. (1981). *Family Therapy Techniques*. Cambridge, MA: Harvard University Press.

Minuchin, S., Montalvo, B., Guerney, B. G., Rosman, B. L., & Schumer, F. (1967). *Families of the Slums*. New York: Basic Books.

Minuchin, S., Rosman, B. L., & Baker, L. (1978). *Psychosomatic Families: Anorexia Nervosa in Context*. Cambridge, MA: Harvard University Press.

Murburg, M., Price, L., & Jalali, B. (1988). Huntington's disease: therapy strategies. *Family Systems Medicine, 6*: 290–303.

O'Shea, M., & Phelps, R. (1985). Multiple family therapy: current status and critical appraisal. *Family Process, 24*: 555–582.

Papp, P. (1980). The Greek Chorus and other techniques of paradoxical therapy. *Family Process, 19*: 45–57.

Plas, J. M. (1986). *Systems Psychology in the Schools*. New York: Pergamon.

Reiss, D., & Costell, R. (1977). The multiple family group as a small society: family regulation of interaction with non-members. *American Journal of Psychiatry, 134*: 21–24.

Scholz, M., & Asen, E. (2001). Multiple family therapy with eating disordered adolescents: concepts and preliminary results. *European Eating Disorders Review, 9*: 33–42.

Schuff, H., & Asen, K. E. (1996). The disturbed parent and the disturbed family. In: M. Goepfert, J. Webster, & M. V. Seeman, (Eds.), *Parental Psychiatric Disorder*. Cambridge: Cambridge University Press.

Selvini Palazzoli, M., Boscolo, L., Cecchin, G., & Prata, G. (1980). The problem of the referring person. *Journal of Marital and Family Therapy, 6*: 3–9.

Slagerman, M., & Yager, J. (1989). Multiple family group treatment for eating disorders: a short term program. *Psychiatric Medicine, 7*: 269–283.

Stevens, A., Garriga, X., & Epstein, C. (1983). Proximity and distance: a technique used by family day unit workers. *Journal of Family Therapy, 5*: 295–305.

Strelnick, A. H. J. (1977). Multiple family group therapy: a review of the literature. *Family Process, 16*: 307–325.

Summer, J. (1998). "Multiple Family Therapy: Its Use in the Assessment and Treatment of Child Abuse. A Pilot Study." Unpublished MSc thesis, Birkbeck College and Institute of Family Therapy.

Sutherland, J. D. (1965). Recent advances in the understanding of small groups, their disorders and treatment. *Psychotherapy and Psychosomatics, 13*: 110–125.

Wattie, M. (1994). Multiple group family therapy. *Journal of Child and Youth Care, 9*: 31–38.

White, M. (1997). *Narratives of Therapists' Lives*. Adelaide: Dulwich Centre Publications.

Wooley, S., & Lewis, K. (1987). Multi-family therapy within an intensive treatment program for bulimia. In J. Harkaway (Ed.), *Eating Disorders: The Family Therapy Collections, Vol. 20*. Rockville, MD: Aspen.

INDEX